ANTIQUE FURNITURE
FOR PLEASURE AND PROFIT

ANTIQUE FURNITURE FOR PLEASURE AND PROFIT

Ronald Pearsall

DAVID & CHARLES
Newton Abbot   London

Page 2 A Victorian bird's-eye maple Davenport, c1850.

Decorative line drawings
Page 7 A military chest in mahogany c1870.
Page 9 A Carlton House writing table in the
Edwardian Sheraton style c1900.
Page 97 A walnut gate-leg table c1680.
Page 169 A Restoration armchair in Walnut c1680.
Page 188 An *indiscret* or conversation sofa c1850.

Author's note
Unless indicated otherwise, furniture prices recorded in the text
and captions refer to sales in 1988.

British Library Cataloguing in Publication Data

Pearsall, Ronald
    Antique furniture for pleasure and profit.
    1. Furniture. Collectors and collecting
    I. Title
    749'.1

    ISBN 0-7153-9387-1

Typeset by Typesetters (Birmingham) Ltd,
Smethwick, West Midlands
and printed in Portugal
for David & Charles plc
Brunel House Newton Abbot Devon

Contents

PART II — THE PRACTICAL ASPECTS 97

Repairing and Restoring your Furniture 98

PART III — APPENDICES 169

Introduction

This book is in three main parts. The first describes in detail the various kinds of furniture and how they all developed; the second part looks at how to improve and enhance the beauty of your antiques; and the third part, the appendices section, provides the kind of useful information the amateur needs in order to go about buying and selling on a small scale. A hobby can turn into a business, a collector can become an antique dealer, and so the list of up-to-date auction prices, on a wide variety of items, is a must for any authoritative book on antiques.

If furniture needs repairing, this book describes how and lists all the tools and materials needed – not only for any work to the wood, but to the upholstery, to any fittings, and to leather. If there is cane or rushwork that needs replacing, that is dealt with too, as are any problems connected with woodworm.

If the furniture needs refurbishing, the information is here (waxing, French polishing, getting rid of burn marks and water stains), but it is never forgotten that antique furniture ought to show signs of wear and tear in order to look truly authentic.

Of course, there is furniture and furniture, and there is certainly furniture on the subject of which no-one can wax lyrical. But even apparently worthless pieces can be transformed by painting, marbling, spattering, sponging and general renovation into something quite original. All these processes are described in detail, and all can be reversed if the going gets tough!

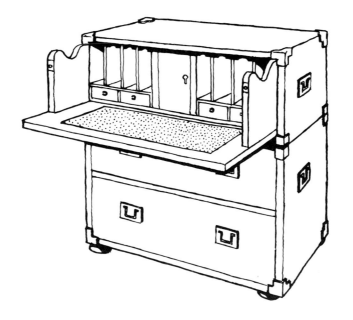

PART I

THE FURNITURE

English Furniture

Furniture is the most personal of all antiques. Lived with, used, it takes on a personality of its own; as with friends, it is treasured despite (or even because of) its imperfections. For true antique furniture is never flawless, and that is part of its appeal.

But there is furniture which does not appeal. It may be good, it may be worthy, but somehow alien to us. It may be the rectangular modernist chairs of the 1920s, made out of four slab-sided pieces of wood and now worth several thousand pounds; or it may be one of those heavily carved Burmese desks that were imported in the days of the British Empire and take four strong men to carry them. Or, to put it bluntly, it may be rubbish, indifferently made and boring. To be of any interest, it needs transforming, and later in the book it will be explained how this can be done.

Furniture developed in a haphazard way: in the early days it was far less important than tapestries and hangings. Before the seventeenth century houses were sparsely furnished. The most common item was the coffer, which held everything, and the aumbry or food cupboard. There were tables, many of them the trestle type, and only the rich sat on chairs. Others used benches and stools. The rich had four-poster beds because they served to display costly draperies; ordinary people slept in beds like boxes or on whatever they could find.

Most of the furniture that survives from the seventeenth century and earlier was made from oak. The furniture made from other woods has mostly rotted away. Oak furniture was often richly carved, was easily worked and took the kind of decoration that was popular, done with gouge and chisel. Construction was basic. The skills were there, but were used for other purposes.

The best furniture was imported, and refugees from religious persecution brought new ideas to Britain. It may appear that much of the furniture before, say, 1700 was unbearably uncomfortable. But the earlier furniture was fitted out with cushions and a form of upholstery. Construction depended on the means available, and the uniting of timbers depended on joints, especially the mortice and tenon. The dovetail joint came later.

About 1670 floral marquetry furniture began to come in from Holland, and was imitated. Walnut was preferred to oak. Lacquer work was imported from Japan, and this was also copied. Elegant gilded furniture was brought in from France, the European cultural centre.

As women became more important in society, they began to demand more in the way of custom-made furniture, and had an important part to play in future developments. To many the new styles seemed alien, far removed from the no-nonsense oak. Chairs were lighter and more fragile, and proliferated in a number of styles, some awkward, some elegant and foreshadowing things to come. In the country there was not the same concern for the little extras of civilised life, and plain oak settles were staple features of the yeoman's farm or house.

A Victorian engraving of an Elizabethan oak bed. Such illustrations are often idealised; this is what a Victorian expected an Elizabethan bed to look like.

With the fashion for totally panelled rooms, wardrobes could be built into the walls, and open cupboards were also fitted into the panelling for the display of china and curios brought back from foreign parts. Among the most varied types of furniture were the side tables, useful and ornamental, and among the most impressive were large two-stage writing cabinets, the bottom part a bureau with a fall-front for writing on, the upper part sometimes used for books.

In 1709 walnut was in short supply. Wood from the British colonies was freed from heavy import duties, and this included mahogany. Although mahogany had been known for some time it was now used as a substitute for walnut, and from 1725 it supplanted it. It was strong, easily polished, did not easily warp, and was resistant to woodworm. It allowed finer carving, and because of its strength it did not need reinforcing with stretchers.

With Thomas Chippendale's *Gentleman and Cabinet-Maker's Directory* of 1754, a guide was provided to what was in fashion. Later Hepplewhite and Sheraton were to provide further books on similar lines, all very influential. Certain trends were encouraged: curved, bowed, serpentine shapes, delicate carving and a general appearance of elegance, especially if it could be spiced with foreign influences or could mirror the current enthusiasm for the Gothic style.

The Neoclassicism associated with the name of Robert Adam made an appearance in the 1760s. Classical ornament, light-coloured wood, and marquetry, were all combined in the new style, which was airy and graceful. A leading proponent was Hepplewhite who endeavoured 'to unite elegance and utility and blend the useful with

Fantasy piece exhibited in 1862 showing the Victorian interpretation of Old England.

the agreeable'. Sheraton popularised simple clean lines, compactness, and furniture that could be used for a variety of purposes.

All this time furniture was being produced in the country in oak, very much along traditional lines – simple furniture such as the Windsor chair (first mentioned in 1724). The dresser was essentially a country piece, and the pine dressers produced in Wales were particularly magnificent.

By the end of the eighteenth century Europe was in turmoil. The French Revolution had sent a wave of fear throughout England. The furniture-makers continued their work, but social conditions were changing, and with them a demand for a new kind of furniture. This was most apparent in France. The Napoleonic regime demanded Napoleonic furniture, and it got it – powerful, strident, massive. And there was a similar trend in Britain, with the Regency period, strictly 1811-20, though its influence was by no means confined to those years.

What characterises Regency furniture? First of all new, exotic and flashy woods such as rosewood, amboyna, and zebra wood; and new shapes – straight lines, unbroken surfaces, low height, and a self-confident chunkiness. New types of furniture evolved – a variety of drawing-room tables and couches for the ladies, library tables and huge study furniture for the men. Many of these types of furniture persisted well into the reign of Victoria, because they were perfect for the task they were made for.

The reign of William IV was short and unassuming. And at first nothing much changed in the Victorian period. The Victorians looked at their furniture heritage, and picked what they liked, altering it to suit their needs. They wanted more comfortable furniture, so they made it; they wanted furniture which could be made by machine, they got that too. Wooden beds were unhygienic; so they made them of iron and brass. Why use wood to make furniture? So they used papier-mâché. And, of course, occasionally they wanted furniture to make the eyes pop out, exhibition furniture, the bigger the better with every surface carved. This was once thought to be typical Victorian furniture; in a hundred years' time the objects in the 1951 Festival of Britain will be thought to represent ordinary design. And how wrong, on both counts.

Much of the furniture seen today in antiques shops, antiques fairs, and auctions is Victorian; a lot has been exported, but it still remains in enormous quantities. Much of it was copied from furniture from the past, and sometimes it is difficult for even experts to tell. A great deal of it is well-made and almost indestructible. And the Victorians could make unassuming furniture which was well-nigh perfect – such as the balloon-back chair, made for half a century. And the variety of it all! The range of seventeenth-century and earlier furniture is small; even the furniture types of the eighteenth century are few in number. But in the second half of the nineteenth century if a piece of furniture was wanted for a specific purpose, it was there. It could be a chair which doubled as a hearing-aid (one upright acted as an ear-trumpet); it could be a foot-stool for someone with gout.

Money was no object. The silliest things were made. And of course there was rubbish in abundance. There were reactions against the rubbish – the Arts and Crafts movement and the return to nature, with furniture plain and unadorned (and expensive); there was Aesthetic furniture, spindly, ebonised, odd; there was a fad for all things oriental, and a vogue for bamboo, believed to represent everything the mysterious East was about. And towards the end, filtering over into the new century, was Art Nouveau, giving rise to an individual, angular style of furniture on the one hand and another opposite style, sinuous and knobbly, which was most popular in France.

The Edwardian period is reckoned as 1900–1914. Strictly speaking, it should be 1901–10. What happened here? A reaction against the Victorians and everything they stood for. A return to the classics – mahogany, satinwood, marquetry, and eighteenth-century restraint; for the garden suburbs and the new middle classes – waxed oak and Ambrose Heal (still a name to conjure with). Of course, there was flashy furniture for the new rich; there always is. After World War I, there was a desire for comfort, chintz, labour-saving devices, and not much in the way of design. Typical of this

Although seeming to be Regency armchairs of about 1810, these were made about 1900. The proportions are good, though perhaps the design of the back may seem a little fussy.

unassuming, amiable furniture was Lloyd Loom furniture in pleasing pastel shades, and still very cheap. But in Europe a spirit of adventure was abroad. Houses were machines for living in, and furniture must be moulded to the body (or, as often happened, the other way around). Fitness-for-function was the war-cry: mechanised production and the use of new materials. Awed young furniture makers discovered plywood.

The British took to it reluctantly, but as it became commercialised, as they saw these streamlined chromium pieces of furniture in hotel lobbies and cinema foyers they grew to like it. We call it Art Deco. They didn't have a name for it, but it was fashionable and has remained so ever since, along with overstuffed sofas, display cabinets with silvered glass, cocktail cabinets which play a tune, and tables which strike out at the knees. These will be the antiques of the future.

The furniture of the past, whether it is antique or not, is probably best understood split up into types. Some of these merge into each other, and are grouped together, as with clothes presses and wardrobes, side cabinets and bookcases, desks and bureaux. The most important groups are tables and chairs; because of their wide variety they are dealt with at length. Some kinds of furniture did not change (if they are mentioned at all in this book it is in passing. For example, pot cupboards could be cylindrical or angular, but not much else can be said about them except that they are mostly in

Opposite, above: A George II oak dresser base of about 1730 with some restoration.
Below: A Regency rosewood chiffonier of about 1815.

mahogany. Much the same can be said about wine coolers, except the more interesting ones on legs. Corner cupboards are dealt with, but not ordinary side cupboards. If they were of any interest, they had developed into something else, such as a cabinet. Wall cupboards could include the early aumbries and hutches with their spindled frontages, but these are rare. Indeed, they are so rare that if one turned up in an attic the finder would not place it in an auction and lay down a deposit on a new house, but put a rabbit in it!

I

Beds

There are two types of bed always in demand: the four-poster, and the brass bed. Many four-posters that come onto the market are seventeenth-century but there is a possibility that they have been lengthened because people are taller today, and as most beds are bought for use this is regarded as acceptable. The reason why there are so many early beds about is that they are automatically handed down the family, and unlike other types of furniture were rarely sold. They were also cherished, polished and cared for, so it is likely that they are in good condition, and as the majority were in oak they have not suffered from woodworm infestation. Unlike old oak that was buffeted about, and often stood on cold damp floors – tables, chairs, and general domestic furniture – the legs do not have the uneven quality resulting from a degree of rot and ill-treatment.

The headboard was usually panelled, carved, arcaded, and often inlaid, and the friezes were often highly decorative, as well as the columns supporting the canopy. These were sometimes intricately turned, with bulbous sections of the kind associated with the court cupboard, and as they had to support a heavy top they were very substantial.

Ordinary people slept in compartments which were hardly more than boxes, and most of the eighteenth-century beds that have survived are superior examples, usually in mahogany. Owing to the nature of the wood and its strength, mahogany beds are often lighter in structure, with elegant pillars for the uprights, sometimes worked with characteristic motifs such as the lotus leaf, ears of wheat, and husks. Many so-called plant stands started as the uprights of mahogany four-posters, with an inconsequential circular top added and a base of some kind, sometimes a platform, sometimes a tripod. In mahogany beds, the base-board was often short, and the space to the canopy was taken up with drapes, which also extended to the floor from the mattress.

French beds were either genuine imports from France or English-made in what was known as the Louis style (without specifying which Louis), often with a carved and arched headboard and footboard of equal height, upholstered in satin or silk. Some were in the form of a gondola, and others were derived from day beds.

There were beds in which a fixed canopy was replaced by a tent-like structure on a pole, and there were heavy orthodox beds, the best of which were in the expensive woods with much carving. In the nineteenth century wooden beds were widely recognised as unhygienic, and although the iron bed tended to be associated with hospitals or workhouses, its brass counterpart proved immensely popular and created

A superior mid-nineteenth-century brass bed exhibited in 1862. Hygienic and functional metal beds had given way to exuberance and decoration.

an important industry in Birmingham. Often the brass fittings are on a structure of iron, giving a superficial gloss. The brass bed has been taken up with enthusiasm in recent years, with reproduction models catering for the demand, and most of these appear very similar to the originals as the working of brass does not alter much.

The bedroom suite – comprising bed, washstand and wardrobe – did much to stabilise bed design, and the Edwardian bed is a decent enough piece of furniture without being adventurous. Naturally, the taste for streamlining and extravagantly figured woods in the Noel Coward period influenced the beds of the time, but most people are more interested in the development of the spring mattress which gradually replaced the feather mattress and led to the compact divan bed. Perhaps round beds, king-size beds, and water beds are the antiques of the future but it is doubtful. However, children's furniture has always been much in demand for use, and cradles especially so, as they cater for the doll-collecting market, and even poorly made examples fetch large sums of money.

The tendency of bed development is to make them more comfortable, culminating in the spring mattress in this 1930s bed.

II

Cabinets and Bookcases

The side cabinets of the early nineteenth century are restrained, charming pieces, with brass latticework, galleries, and sometimes marble tops, but they were basically show-pieces and as cabinet merged into credenza there was no end to the ingenuity in covering the surfaces. However, there was a fairly established format for the basic design – a central door, with shelves at the side, sometimes glazed, sometimes curved. In some examples there was a strong French influence. The top was flat, without gallery or protrusion. Marquetry, inset plaques, pillars turned or carved, sometimes in the Egyptian style with lotus motifs – there was a plethora of decorative possibilities, often focussed on the central door. The quality of this work is usually of the highest standard, and every kind of prestige wood was used.

The credenza might well be the key piece of Victorian furniture. Side cabinets of the Aesthetic period (the 1870s and 1880s) have their own individuality. Mirrors were sometimes fitted, and many were ebonised rather than being decorated with flashy inlay. The tops were not often flat, as in the credenza, but usually had superstructures,

Although this has the appearance of a George III secretaire bookcase it was made about 1900. Because of its high quality it still made £18,150 at auction.

18

A classic mid-Victorian chiffonier with firm ornament and expanses of plain wood. In a few years the fashion for decorating such areas would be impossible to resist.

a brass or spindle gallery, or were stepped with the central section higher than the two side portions, or vice versa.

The side cabinet merged into the display cabinet. This answered a need for the multitude of odds and ends the Victorians accumulated, and complemented the whatnots. Cabinets with glass doors could be small and unassuming, with two shelves with leather facings for music, vitrines, mostly glass, or the most incredible creations, referred to contemptuously as Louis monstrosities, and much undervalued. These florid overwhelming pieces, often ebonised, can contain a multitude of different shaped mirrors, a large assortment of shelves and cupboards, some open, some glazed. They may be an acquired taste, but the quality of the inlay, the tortuous arrangement of glazing bars, the rococo fretwork, are often superb, and the craftsmanship which went into these features should be appreciated. They are not objects for box-dwellers, and it is their loss. If seen, and in good condition, buy, and buy now. These are the very expensive antiques of the 1990s.

Art Nouveau had a powerful influence on display cabinets of the early years of the twentieth century: sinuous curving, whiplash inlay, asymmetrical decoration that makes the wood look like sagging plasticine, and a liking for leaded glazing, the panes of glass arranged in small squares. Some had flat-capped uprights, and the inimitable flat feet on slender supports, which give a misleading impression of fragility. Many of these cabinets were made, but in numbers were probably far fewer than routine reproductions and rough interpretations of what Sheraton or Chippendale would have done had they been asked to produce one (for the display cabinet is hardly a classic eighteenth-century product).

After many years when they were just dumped, display cabinets of the 1920s and 1930s are now in demand. Basically they are simple, with sun-burst motifs in the glazing bars and silvered decoration on the glass, a device used to excess in period cocktail cabinets. Cabriole legs were much used in these cabinets. There must be millions of them about, the home of seaside souvenirs with the top as the obvious place for framed photographs. As with Edwardian reproduction furniture, they are not all of a piece. Some are high quality, made for people who wished to display Dresden rather than china carthorses.

The display cabinet was the logical successor to the Victorian side cabinet. The chiffonier, on the other hand, had few descendants. The chiffonier is a side cabinet with an upper shelf or shelves, with grille front, often curtained with silk, and perhaps with brass fittings and galleries. Throughout the nineteenth century it preserved a certain decorum, though the later ones often tended to be more functional with shabby machine-carved backs and made in cheap wood. Some had drawers, some did not. They are useful pieces, often used nowadays as bookcases. Some of them can unquestionably be classified as boarding-house furniture where the bacon and eggs were left to go cold and jellified.

A close relation of the side cabinet is the bookcase, first mentioned as an item of furniture by Samuel Pepys in his diary. Bookcases, whether small and elegant, part of a bureau bookcase, whether breakfront (where the central section of three juts out), or massive Victorian Gothic, have always been expensive and mainly bought for use by book-lovers, who never have enough storage space for their treasures. Large plain bookcases, with panelled doors beneath, were made without change for more than half a century because they did the job they had to do perfectly. As they were

21

REGENCY ROSEWOOD CHIFFONIER

1 Check that the brass gallery is intact. A repair will devalue the piece, but not to a great extent. If a section of the gallery is missing a replacement can be cut from brass plate, using a good section of the gallery as a model (use tracing paper to follow the lines). A metal-worker will be able to fit in a new section so that it does not show, but gluing may suffice though it will not convince the experts. When putting in a new section make certain that it is blended down to match the old brass.

2 See that the inlay is all there, and check that there are no repairs.

3 There may or may not be a lock. If there is some doubt about it being in period look carefully for screw holes on the inside of the door that seem to indicate a replacement lock. Look at the part of the door where the bolt slides in. Has wood been filled in or taken out to accommodate a different bolt?

4 Are the feet in period? Bracket feet would be anachronistic, bun feet a possible Victorian substitution. Look underneath to see if there are any unexplained screw holes, and check that the bottoms of the feet are worn; there is always the possibility that the feet are modern reproduction, which would not of course have natural wear, though unscrupulous dealers may try to age substitute feet by filing or sanding and rubbing dirt into the wood.

5 Do the finials match, and are they in keeping? Is there any damage to the brass supports which, being hollow and not solid, are subject to denting? This can often be detected by running the hand up the support rather than trusting the eye.

6 Is the mirror in good condition, or is there a brown tinge, indicative that the silvering is not good? A crackling effect is also proof of deterioration. Old glass was thinner than modern glass: hold the thumb nail against the glass and look at the reflection; the distance between the real nail and the reflected nail represents the thickness of the mirror.

7 Look at the back of the chiffonier. As it is an against-the-wall piece there may be some crudity in the finish, but if there has been any woodworm it will show up more clearly here. Also look at where the mirror top is fixed to the base, and see if it looks a sensible arrangement. If there are unexplained light or dark patches in the wood, it may possibly indicate that the top and the bottom do not belong, though in a piece of this character it is not likely as anachronisms are usually glaringly obvious.

8 The shelves may be lined, and if the material is period it may have suffered damage from moths or general decay. This is not important, and if a substitute material has been provided this does not detract from the value of the piece of furniture.

9 See that there is no split in the mahogany top which may indicate overall warping. If there is, assess the difficulty of repair. A split may need a sliver of veneer, or may be filled with wax. This is not a difficult operation, but if the chiffonier is nicely polished it may be time-consuming to bring a newly treated top to a good matching finish.

---

often gentlemen's and study furniture, superfluous ornamentation was kept to a minimum. In the more ornate examples, with tricky glazing bar design, there may be some doubt as to whether the piece of furniture is a bookcase or a display cabinet.

The low open bookshelf was a favourite item of furniture in the cultured Edwardian home, in plain oak, with period motifs punched through the side uprights (hearts, tulips etc). Some of the divisions were low in height to house the products of the Everyman Library and the Collins Classics, then published for the first time. This sort of bookshelf, suitably streamlined, has continued to be made until the present day. It is the kind of functional furniture that would have been understood in the seventeenth century and earlier by the joiners who made stools.

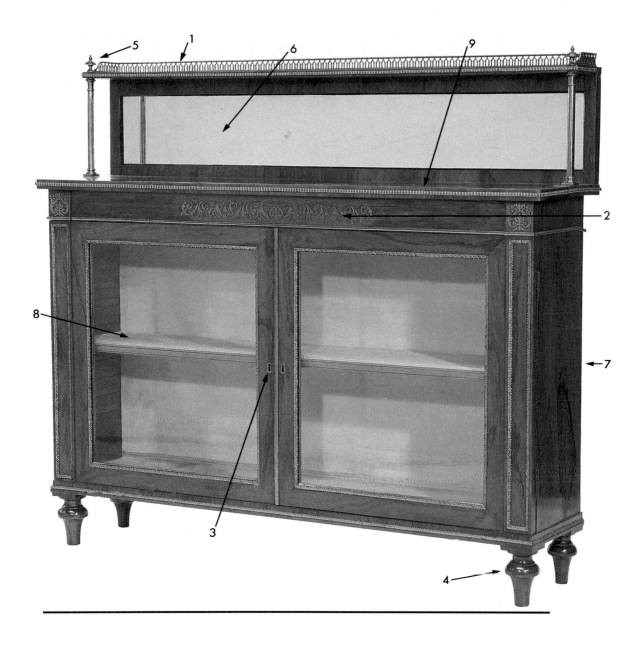

Art Deco bookcases with a bureau facility cannot by any stretch of the imagination be termed bureau bookcases. They are usually very angular, and the bureau fittings are often restricted to pigeon-holes. Squat and compact, they have a restricted usage. As low-cost furniture they may have potential for transformation, or a role in the nursery or playroom.

Revolving bookcases, usually in mahogany, have always been in demand. They are not a particularly useful piece of furniture, as they hold a limited number of books, but as they are becoming increasingly difficult to purchase at auction, they are pieces which are much sought-after by antique dealers and owners of a few choice first editions.

An early eighteenth-century bureau-cabinet on bracket feet. In the opinion of many experts, any imperfections in such a piece should be left as they are.

III

Canterburies

The Canterbury is now highly rated as a fashionable and decorative piece of furniture in which to put music, magazines or newspapers, but at the end of the eighteenth century it was no more than a tea trolley, and referred to as such by Sheraton. The music Canterbury dates from about 1800 and originally was of austere rectangular shape with the sides and partitions of simple open fret, with turned or carved posts extending below the base to form legs, usually slotted into castors. There was often a shallow drawer for sheet music. The partition top rails were slightly rounded with a central dip to allow for the easy withdrawal of music.

Many woods were used – mahogany, rosewood, walnut and satinwood. The Regency favoured diagonal latticework between square-cut rails, claw feet, lyre motifs, emphasising the musical connection. During the Victorian period the outer partitions were intricately fretted, and most were on ornately turned legs, invariably with castors so that they could be moved around and slid under the grand piano if not wanted. Papier-mâché Canterburies were made, but are quite rare, unlike the bamboo Canterburies of the Aesthetic period which often have lacquer panels and have little to commend them.

Sometimes a writing slope was added to the top, which would seem to mean that the Canterbury was also used for notepaper and envelopes, and the Canterbury could match the whatnot (or omnium). Most carving on Canterburies is of high quality, and where a top is provided it is often fitted out with a brass gallery. It was never a particularly useful piece of furniture, for its capacity was limited; the average Canterbury would take the Beethoven piano sonatas and that was it. The shelved

There are only a few types of furniture, then there are the 'fancies' such as Canterburies and then the curios, spin-offs from standard types such as this Victorian acoustic chair.

25

A fine breakfront bookcase of about 1880, a lesson to anyone who believes that the Victorians had no appreciation of proportions though the marquetry pictures indicate the period.

music cabinet or the hinged-top piano stool were much more practical, as most music is in flimsy covers, so placing it upright would damage and crease it in very little time. The popularity of the Canterbury lay not in what it did, but in what it was – a well-made decorative piece of furniture in fashionable wood.

There are no problems in buying a Canterbury. There are no hidden perils. Look for quality of carving and fretwork, examining the fretwork closely to make certain that there are no bits missing – not so easy when the fretwork is manic. Make certain that the castors are intact and that they all 'belong', ie there are no replacements. Also ascertain that there are the right number of partitions (a damaged member might have been taken out). Most Canterburies have three or four divisions, but there are exceptions.

Regency Canterburies will most likely have brass handles to any drawer there may be. Victorian specimens generally have small bun handles, though these may have been replaced in the interests of fashion.

As with Canterburies, the bonheur-du-jour was a woman's piece, somewhat impractical with an annoyingly small working surface.

IV

Chairs, Sofas and Settles

Early chairs were impressive, like heavy thrones with marquetry, deep carving and inlay. They had decorative and extravagant head-pieces, and the arms led down, usually projecting past the uprights. Stretchers were near the ground. In the 1650s chairs were lighter, upholstered, or caned. The back cross-pieces were covered in leather and studded. Chairs had bobbin legs and stretchers. The Dutch-inspired chairs that followed the restoration of the monarchy were often of grotesque appearance, with excess unnecessary ornamentation. The evolution of the cabriole leg brought some restraint and elegance.

Early eighteenth-century chairs had a central solid splat, sometimes pierced. The main development was in the splat, which became a decorative feature, often intricately divided. This trend was associated with the influence of Chippendale, and the unquestioned beauty and elegance of eighteenth-century chairs was furthered by designers such as Hepplewhite and Sheraton. It is difficult to find a really ugly eighteenth-century chair, whether it be made in London, the provinces, or the country. It was as though there was an instinct for what was right and proper.

They all had their specialities. Hepplewhite made fashionable camel backs and hoop backs, serpentine fronts, the Prince of Wales plumes as a design motif, tapering fluted legs, and leaf and swag carving. Chippendale made furniture based on popular Gothic and Chinese motifs for the rich who had a taste for the exotic. Cabriole legs and square legs were both used, sometimes terminating in a ball-and-claw foot, believed to be of Chinese origin. With Sheraton we bridge the gap with the nineteenth century; he was sometimes idiosyncratic (he later became deranged), and sometimes deceptively simple. Designs without carving or excess ornament continued to be produced by traditional country carpenters.

English chair design in the eighteenth century was the most progressive in Europe, and had a great influence on European chairs. High quality chairs were often roughly finished off at the back. This was not idleness or poor workmanship, but was due to the fact that in grand houses chairs stood against the wall. By the end of the century the centres of rooms were no longer left clear, so chairs had to be finished all round.

There was a profusion of designs. It was as though there was no end to the variations possible. Certain themes recur, and are worked through. The turned leg once again became popular, and a new type of leg was produced, the sabre leg, structurally unsound because the wood was cut against the grain. One of the most delightful variants was the reeded leg of the William IV period and later.

Chairs with arms and upholstered chairs are more expensive than those without. Seventeenth-century upholstered chairs are straight-backed and not the last word in comfort, but when the wing chair appeared, it proved to be a classic design. Upholstered chairs with open arms or no arms at all were made in a wide variety of styles, often only datable by the legs and by the presence of original upholstery. There was a demand for an easy chair of elegance, and this was provided by giltwood neo-classical designs, continually reproduced ever since. One of the most charming easy chairs was the French-influenced bergère, with caned sides and/or back, often in a suite.

The classic Victorian dining room chair, the balloon-back, an elegant example from about 1850.

Chairs with a diagonal seat are corner chairs, sometimes known as writing chairs. They have low backs and are not common, and the ones most often seen are Edwardian reproductions.

More chairs were made than any other piece of furniture. They are therefore more common, but they are also the most vulnerable to damage. They are never to be taken on trust; if you are buying a set of chairs examine each one with equal attention. If it is a 'long' set, it may be that damage is spread out amongst the chairs. Check that the splats have not been repaired, or worse, replaced.

What did the Victorians do with the chair? First of all they reproduced traditional designs they liked best, and then they made their own amendments. They found the Chippendale square leg too chunky so they refined it; they did not care for the large square seat, so they made it smaller. Many of the Victorian reproduction chairs are excellent; it needs an expert to tell an original from a good Victorian re-creation. But there are some chairs and other furniture where there is no doubt about the date, as in the Gothic style. In A. W. N. Pugin's words:

We find diminutive flying buttresses about an armchair, everything is crocketed with angular projections, innumerable mitres, sharp ornaments and turreted extremities. A man who remains any length of time in a modern Gothic room and escapes without becoming wounded by some of its minutiae may consider himself fortunate.

REGENCY LIBRARY STEPS AND CHAIR

1 Dual-purpose furniture is often neither one thing nor the other, and although this Regency chair combined with library steps is a superior example the steps themselves are quite short, though with their aid a person could reach the top shelf of a bookcase. Check that the hinges which turn the chair into steps are in order. They may need rescrewing or resetting if the chair has actually been used as a pair of steps, which is by no means certain.

2 The top rail slots into the uprights, and if the rail needs repair it can be taken out easily.

3 If there is damage it may be a considerable job to put right, except to a professional, because of the curvature and the reeding. A break, however, is not likely in a chair of this form.

4 The terminals to the arms are to a certain degree vulnerable, because the direction of the mahogany grain means that there is always the chance of a clean snap. As there is no pressure on these, gluing will suffice, and with mahogany there will be no awkward positioning when the piece is replaced. A light polishing will camouflage any repair.

5 When checking the caning turn the chair upside down to see what is happening there. Make certain that there is no weakness where the caning abuts the wood. Caning is not difficult to do (see the appropriate section in the book) but it is time-consuming, and to have the chair recaned in the present 'superior' style is very expensive. If a small section is damaged, weigh up the possibility of just doing that section and integrating it with the good section, bearing in mind that the canework is in one section and bears the full weight of the person sitting on it.

6 Sabre legs are slightly at risk because of the grain, but if they break it is usually a clean break and the chances are that it would occur below the stretchers and not above. The reeding is an asset rather than a hindrance as it will act as a placement guide when the repair is made. A repair would have to be sturdy, perhaps using two dowels, because the front legs bear considerable pressure.

7 Dirt and grime build up in the grooves of the reeding, and with the addition of polish can be converted into a hard substance that may need rigorous treatment in getting out. A solvent may prove sufficient, but mahogany is a hardy wood and if probing and scraping are necessary any bruising can be put right.

Some of the most endearing Victorian furniture is that in which styles of the past are jumbled together. Sir Walter Scott's novels were very popular at the time, and when Queen Victoria bought Balmoral, there was a craze for all things Scottish, manifested in pebble jewellery, tartan novelties, and what was known as Abbotsford furniture, vaguely baronial but not very Scottish.

The typical own-brand Victorian chair, disregarding eccentricities, is the balloon-back, with straight legs, turned with slightly bulbous knobs at the top. The first tentative designs had a dipped top rail, not yet a full balloon. The first indication of the balloon-back chair occurs in 1833; in 1840 it was referred to as a parlour chair. It was strong, reliable, and there was no nonsense about it. It was made in quantity for many decades, and the rounded rail was much used in upholstered chairs, especially the buttoned-backs. Of course, the balloon-back was only one of many dining chairs (a convenient description covering a multitude of uses except purely decorative). There were chairs with caned backs, chairs with arched galleries, innumerable chairs with spindles, either in a neat row, or grouped en-masse, downright ugly chairs with low-level incised carving, known as 'scratch' decoration, sometimes with boxwood inlay to emphasise the mean quality. Nevertheless, if these chairs are in sets they are in demand.

A Victorian patent action button-back rosewood chair with a fold-under footstool, illustrating the interest and sometimes obsession with dual-purpose furniture.

Victorian upholstered chairs, with or without arms, go by a number of names such as nursing chairs and ladies' chairs. There is an immense variety, some splendid carving, and some breezy design. They are often very comfortable, often thanks to the invention of the spiral spring, which influenced seat shapes. A distinctive Victorian upholstered chair is the prie-dieu or vespers, with low dumpy legs, a high back, and very popular as a display piece for Berlin woolwork and home embroidery. Sometimes the ornamentation on upholstered chairs may seem excessive. There was a reaction against self-indulgent comfort in the 1870s, and furniture reflected this. There was a revival of eighteenth-century styles and this continued into the Edwardian period, with a welter of plain but pleasant mass-produced dining chairs, and some very likeable occasional chairs with padded seats and ingenious variations in the backs, using Art Nouveau motifs brought into common life. After World War I the pursuit of comfort was paramount. Furniture was chintzy, stuffed, until the frames of chairs were lost in the billowing upholstery.

There is nothing excessive about the best-known country chair of all time, the Windsor, first recorded in 1724, which continued in a multitude of varieties. They are mostly made from ash or yew, with elm seats.

Until about 1780 legs were tenoned and wedged into mortice holes bored right through the seat. After this the spoon bit was used, which had no point, so a deep hole could be bored without coming through the top of the seat. Legs were turned or whittled, and cabriole legs were only used on Windsors of the highest quality. The usual stretchers were 'H'-shaped, with two stretchers linking back and front. In the 1750s the crinoline or cow's horn stretcher in the form of an arc was used, and chairs which have this feature are highly valued.

The splat was first solid, vase- or fiddle-shaped, and this was followed by pierced designs. The well-known wheel pattern came at the end of the eighteenth century. The low-backed smoker's bow was introduced about 1830, and made almost without change for a hundred years or more.

Naturally Windsors were only one type of country chair. There are dozens of other varieties without fancy names, designated by their construction – ladder-backs, with horizontal splats, often fanciful, mainly from the north of England and the Midlands; spindle-backs, chairs echoing Sheraton's designs, sometimes with elegant turned and reeded horizontal splats that look as though they should belong to London chairs. Sometimes they are scorned as institutional chairs; at best they are 'kitchen chairs', excepting the Arts and Crafts chairs, produced by men such as William Morris, who went back to nature and provided chairs which he thought those who were able to buy from him (the very rich) ought to sit on, for their souls' sake:

> I say our furniture should be good citizens' furniture, solid and well made in workmanship and in design should have nothing about it that is not easily defensible, no monstrosities or extravagances, not even of beauty, lest we weary of it.

Certain Arts and Crafts chairs have a marvellous distinction; they can be recognised from a distance by their overall shape, difficult to define but inimitable. At one end of the spectrum are plain functional chairs, unconsciously used as models during the World War II period when utility chairs were the only ones made. At the other are the chairs designed by Charles Rennie Mackintosh and other designers now so popular, a world apart from almost everything else that was being made at the time.

Country chair-makers often worked in a team. One did seats, one did stretchers, one did legs. The output of a rural workshop was maybe twelve singles and four carvers a week. The traditional wood was ash, but they also worked in yew, sycamore, birch, oak, beech, and the fruitwoods – in fact, any local tree that was handy. The main technological aid was the foot-operated pole lathe with a bent sapling as the source of power.

Why was the north of England such a centre of country chairs? As a direct result of industrialisation, there was a demand for utilitarian furniture in the new towns of Lancashire and Yorkshire, and agricultural workers uprooted from their native homes turned to furniture-making. In Lancashire there were 20 known workshops in 1790; in 1816 there were 41. Pole lathes gave way to treadle and belt-driven lathes, increasing production capacity. If country chairs were comfortable and a farmer could lean back on the rear legs without fear that the structure would collapse under him, the hall chair was the ultimate in discomfort. They usually have flat hard seats. The solid or pierced backs often feature coats of arms, monograms, or whimsical designs to amuse the lower-class person sitting on the chairs. They have something in common with children's chairs, especially those named after Ashley Cooper. These were designed 'with a view to preventing children from acquiring the habit of leaning

One of a set of eight Regency mahogany sabre-legged chairs with characteristic reeded back supports.

VICTORIAN ROSEWOOD BALLOON-BACK CHAIR

1 One of the most indestructible types of chair, this Victorian balloon back is in rosewood, so any major repairs would entail getting hold of this kind of wood and matching the inimitable grain. As with all cabriole-leg furniture the ankle of the leg is the most vulnerable. If it snaps off with the grain, it may be possible to run a long screw upwards through the base of the foot. An alternative method is to insert a dowel.

2 The back legs, being sabre type, may also crack with the grain, though this is improbable. If this does happen, inserting a dowel or dowels is an easier operation because of the shape of the leg and greater ease in putting the leg into a vice.

3 The oval splat is stuffed, probably with horse hair though the original material may have been replaced with kapok or something else. If the velvet covering is ragged it may need to be replaced, and if this is done a cheaper substitute such as velveteen should not be used as a high quality chair such as this deserves the best. There should be no difficulty in slotting back the oval into its wooden surround.

4 If possible during renovation of the oval splat the braid should be reused. If new braid is used it means redoing the trim of the seat as it is unlikely that a match will be found for the original braid.

5 If there is a break in the cresting rails, or a piece of the ornament has snapped off, a potential buyer must have serious doubts about the advisability of purchase, especially if the broken-off piece is missing and there is no chance of gluing it back on. A new piece could be carved and glued back on – as there is no pressure on it gluing would be sufficient – but again the grain would need to be matched.

6 When buying, check beneath the seat to see what the condition is like. If recovering, the braid will help keep the operation tidy. It will be noted that the path of the braid follows the contours of the wood.

7 The knees of the chair are the most subject to general wear, and each should be closely examined to see if there is bruising, chipping or scratching, all of which can be put right without problems.

NINETEENTH-CENTURY WINDSOR CHAIR

1 If slats are loose, squeeze glue into the bottom socket only so that there is a degree of flexibility. If a slat is broken and needs replacing it may be possible to fit in a new one by forcing it in, though the dismantling of a Windsor chair is not difficult. A new slat can be made from a length of dowelling using a spokeshave to get the taper.

2 Although a hooped stretcher adds value to a Windsor chair, it is a potential breaking point because it is held under tension. Making a replacement means acquiring the art of making bentwood furniture (bending the moist wood in steam), perhaps beyond the capabilities of an amateur without equipment.

3 Naturally Windsor chairs are being made today without intent to deceive in exactly the same fashion as they were more than 150 years ago. But it is always possible that modern ones will be passed off as old ones. Look for genuine signs of wear at places where wear occurs – at the bottom of the legs, where the arms protrude. Old Windsor seats were most probably shaped with an adze, resulting in an uneven surface quality, and if the seat is made too perfectly it may mean – though this is not certain – the use of modern tools.

4 Look beneath the seat. It should be rough, left as it is, and fairly clean. If it has been begrimed a misguided faker may have been at work.

5 Some splats are simple; some, as in this case, echo the splats of fine furniture. If damaged they can be taken out quite easily, and a new section put in. As the depth of the wood is usually the same, a new place can be cut with a coping saw or a fretsaw, using an existing section as a pattern. If the edge of the new piece is tapered, and the edge of the old section tapered to match, it will give purchase when the glue is applied. The splat may be too thin to make a really substantial repair. If it is a low value chair, a damaged splat can be recarved so that both sides match.

6 A turned leg of this nature is very strong, and a break is rare. Because of its symmetry, a turned leg is more easily dowelled than one of the fancy legs.

7 A replacement stretcher may perhaps be forced in, as with one of the slats, but if the stretcher bellies out, the carving may present a slight problem – unless the repairer has the use of a lathe.

An Art Deco sofa of about 1930, illustrating admirably the interest in streamlining.

forward, or stooping; the upright position of the back affording support when the child is placed at table, and eating, which a sloped backed chair does not.' The chairs of more disciplined children were the miniatures of adults': sometimes they had a rocking facility; sometimes they were in two parts, with springs between.

In about 1830 Michael Thonet of Vienna had discovered that moist beechwood could be steamed and bent into a circular shape, eliminating joints completely, and by the 1850s bentwood furniture was immensely popular in England, especially for use in restaurants, clubs and hotels. Heal's used bentwood for campaign tables and chairs: 'The peculiar advantage of the above equipment is that it can all be packed on the back of a horse or mule'. A light bentwood saddle was provided. It was copied in metal for rocking chairs, and in the 1920s and 1930s the shape was revived in chrome and other polished metals.

The designs of chairs influenced those of sofas and settees. The difference between sofa and settee (derived from settle) is largely one of size. Originally the sofa was larger and more comfortable. The sopha was the couch, raised on a dais covered with cushions, on which Grand Vizier sat to receive guests. They could be known as confidantes. Adam designed one in 1780, and the sofa was illustrated by Hepplewhite in 1788. A typical example had a seat at each end, with a separated upholstered division. The sociable was an 'S' shape or centre piece. Love seats and courting chairs are merely chairs with wide seats, and the names have been wished on to them by enterprising dealers.

The Italian version of the chest, the cassone, had a back added to it as early as the sixteenth century, and became the cassapanca or hall seat. The English box-seated settle was one variation. The earliest were probably fitted close to fireplaces as built-in furniture, high and box-like to exclude draughts. They were panelled, with box seats and bobbin-turned arm supports. The bacon settle was very tall, and contained cupboards to hang bacon, made in oak, ash, elm, and pine. There were often up to three drawers in the base.

Eighteenth-century settees were often two or three chairs linked together, and it shows. Another type is the Knole settee, with hinged arms, named after the location near Sevenoaks in Kent. The classical couch or day bed, a favourite French piece of furniture, provided a much more interesting scenario, leading to the chaise-longue and the convoluted Victorian settee in all its glory, a piece of furniture that to many sums up Victorian design and is certainly the most easily dated piece of furniture ever made. Chaise-longues of the 1880s onwards are not so endearing, with their endless spindles. The chaise-longue was mentioned by Sheraton in 1791: 'These have their names from the French, which imports a long chair. Their use is to rest or loll upon after dinner.' The late-Victorian chaise-longue would have resisted any lolling. Its shape tended to throw its occupants onto the floor.

The male settee or sofa is unquestionably the Chesterfield, often buttoned, usually refurbished in leather. There is very little a Victorian designer could do with the shape of the Chesterfield except perhaps add ornamental pillars to the two ends, and modern Chesterfields are not much different to those made 120 years ago.

After World War I, we have on the one hand mass-produced chain-store furniture with rexine seats and meaningless low-relief ornament, and on the other, a realisation that new methods and new materials could revolutionise design. Wood was liable to warp. 'The laminated structure of plywood, with its counterstress of grain, has largely obviated this disadvantage in the material', wrote Herbert Read. Bentwood, using damp heat, was also widely used, as well as steel tube, which 'is more durable and brighter'.

Scorn was poured on chintzy comfort; easy chairs represented 'some of the ugliest and most shapeless forms ever devised by man'. Metal furniture of the 1920s and 1930s can fetch fantastic prices at auction, but beware: modern office furniture bears more than a superficial resemblance to even the best pieces. History is repeating itself; just as Edwardian reproduction furniture can be mistaken for the real thing (and vice versa!) so can the fitness-for-function products of adventurous designers (many of them European) be confused with objects made yesterday.

V

Chests and Chests of Drawers

Chests were once the most important pieces of furniture in the house. The earliest form was a hollowed-out tree trunk (a type made up to the seventeenth century), but by the thirteenth century chests were made with simple carved decoration and hinged lids which could be locked. Medieval chests were often banded with iron. Chests with rounded arches are known as Romanesque. Early examples were on a massive scale with boards housed into wide uprights known as stiles. The French favoured very elaborate carving or scrollwork in iron, Britain preferred simple chip carving of roundels. The Spanish used geometric carving strongly influenced by Islam. Italian chests were sometimes sarcophagus-shaped, sometimes rectangular, with carving or painting on gesso ground.

In the 1960s there was a vogue for early Spanish chests in solid walnut and they were being imported in great quantities. Because of their simplicity and lack of sophistication they were being made in the self-same manner by cottage industries in Spain.

The simplest chests were plank coffers: boards nailed onto slab ends. There was no framework, just front, back, ends, and lid, hinged or fitting loosely into slots in the interior of the back. There were sometimes iron carrying handles at the ends, but these were largely continental in origin. The sides could extend past the body of the chest and act as legs. In the late fifteenth century thin panels were set loosely in the chests (to reduce the impact of shrinkage of wood). The ornamentation on these panels is known as linenfold, because they were carved to imitate folded cloth. Linenfold panelling, discreet and simple, gave way to carving, which could be restrained and stylish, or bold and adventurous, mostly non-figurative though sometimes naturalistic features occur, often with a curious Celtic feel. The tops of chests were either plain or in the form of panels.

Nails were used in the manufacture of chests, but these chests disintegrated because the nails rusted. For a time, two types of hinges were popular, the wire hinge (two interlocking loops of wire) and the strap hinge, made in two parts, a short broad part on the wood which remains stationary, and a long often ornate tongue on, for example, the lid of a chest. Strong and reliable, the strap hinge continued to be used after the wire hinge had been dropped, and for many articles of furniture it has not been bettered. For more delicate use, the butterfly hinge came in at the end of the seventeenth century.

Because they were portable, and the great landowners took their furniture with them when they moved from castle to castle, valuables were kept in the chests, which sometimes had intricate locks. Church chests had three locks, one for the priest, one each for the church wardens, and none of the keys was interchangeable. Locks on old chests are sometimes a problem; they sometimes lock themselves. But if the lid is pushed forcibly to one side the lock is usually disengaged.

As the development of the ordinary chest proceeded there were specialised usages, such as dower chests, and domed trunks for travel. The domed trunks are less valuable than those with a flat top. Some of these are made in leather, well-studded, sometimes with vestiges of hair still in evidence, but they are often in a deplorable condition and very little can be done with them.

Inlay came in, and there was a delight in seeing the effect of contrasting woods as well as inlay of ivory, bone, and mother-of-pearl. In the seventeenth century chests were made with drawers. They were beginning to develop into something else, the chest of drawers, and similar carcase furniture. Drawers were first grooved in the thick sides to run on bearers fixed to the carcase frame inside the chest, but after about 1660 the bottom runner, which required a bearer or lining below the drawer, was used. The one-compartment chest continued to be made, sometimes set on a stand. Some of these were elaborate with cabriole legs incorporating shell motifs and ball-and-claw feet or fluted tapering square-section legs with spade feet.

The weight of these chests was often too much for the stands, which consequently collapsed, and there was a trade in providing replacements. These are known as Hackney Road after the main area of their manufacture. Sometimes legs were replaced by bun feet, a practice that is quite acceptable. The most vulnerable were cabriole legs, particularly in walnut.

Regarding old chests, original fitments are very desirable, though in many cases hinges have rusted off and have been replaced: this is quite easy to see as replacement hinges can rarely have matched the original and there will be indications in the form of screw holes or wood discolouration. Locks are frequently missing, and, unlike hinges, there has been less inclination to replace them.

It is often difficult to distinguish between original carving and Victorian embellishment. The Victorians often carved figures in the open arches of genuine antique chests. A favourite motif in sixteenth-century chests was the lozenge, and many Victorian improvers found this irresistible. Of course, one-compartment chests have continued to be made, many of them basic to serve a utilitarian purpose. The larger ones often lend themselves to being upholstered, whereupon they miraculously turn into ottomans and are worth considerably more than they were as common chests.

Between 1650 and 1680 mitred geometrical mouldings and split balusters were applied to the chest, and sets of drawers were often concealed behind doors. After walnut, where a good deal of faking occurs, lacquer, and marquetry came mahogany chests. The best walnut chests have the top veneered with four consecutive veneer sheets to make a pattern. Oak was still used in simple eighteenth-century country chests, and these were often crossbanded with mahogany. In tune with fashion, chests of drawers began to have serpentine, bow and concave fronts.

A George I walnut
tallboy with fine figuring.

There is immense variety in chests of drawers, chests-on-stands, chests-on-chests (sometimes called tallboys), bachelors' chests with a folding top and sometimes false drawers down one side, maidens' cabinets, commodes (the French name for chests of drawers); and because of their usefulness and lack of pretence they are always in demand, though gargantuan Victorian specimens are still undervalued. Unlike some items of furniture it is easy to weigh up the pros and cons, though some pieces of furniture have been split. If a chest of drawers has three small drawers on top it is possible that this is the top half of a chest-on-chest. Chests-on-stands were not veneered on top, the reason being that the top was too high to be seen. So a chest with an unaccountably newly veneered top may very well have once stood on a stand.

41

Above: An Elizabeth I oak and inlaid mule chest described as 'reconstructed'. The degree of authenticity is debatable. The decoration is certainly very busy – too busy for comfort.

A good deal of deliberation may be needed to decide if the handles are original, and even experts may differ. Far more importance seems to be given to this question than seems justified. If they are in keeping, and are not obvious modern chain-store replicas, they should be accepted, unless they are Victorian knobs attached to a mahogany chest which cries out for brass handles of some kind. When buying a chest of drawers or similar object all the drawers should be removed to see if there is any binding or if there are broken bits inside. Minor damage to the outside may be overlooked, and where this is the case fragments which have broken off or small pieces of moulding are often automatically popped inside a convenient drawer. Nor should missing keys be regarded as a reason for turning down an otherwise suitable chest of drawers. The locks are mostly standard simple locks and keys are not difficult to come by. Every antique dealer has a stock of old keys for such eventualities.

Military chests, sometimes called campaign chests, are reproduced on a very large scale. The main feature is that there are no protrusions and vulnerable parts are

JAMES I OAK CHEST

1 With a piece of furniture of this age a split across the top can be the rule rather than the exception, and it should not be repaired or camouflaged in any way.

2 When chests were plain it was the custom of the Victorians to add carving, and sometimes it is not easy to determine which is original carving and which has been added later. If the carving is clumsy it is more likely to be Victorian, as it was believed that the makers of chests were fairly simple characters without sophistication. The carving on this genuine piece is free and unselfconscious, and it doesn't matter that the two sides don't quite match.

3 Because of the large amounts these very basic chests fetch at auction – in this case £4,180 – the fakers are much in evidence. There is often a clue in the side pieces. Originals would have been cut with a handsaw (straight marks) not a circular saw (slightly rounded marks). If there are sharp edges it usually indicates lack of wear, but beware as sometimes wood on a face piece is chamfered down.

4 The feet should have signs of wear, even decay. Such chests were often placed on damp stone floors, particularly fairly plain ones, made for hard use and not for show.

5 There are two iron locks on this chest, which may indicate that it was for a church. The priest would have held one key, a church warden the other. Old chests sometimes have a tendency to lock themselves; if the top is yanked roughly to one side it can disengage the lock. Many ancient chests have long since lost their locks, and although this is a pity and a minus point, a missing lock should never be replaced – even with one that could possibly be in period.

6 The lid could be fixed to the chest with a wire hinge (loops of wire), or a strap hinge with a short part on the piece of furniture which is stationary and a long, often ornate tongue on the moving part, in this case the lid. Any other kind of hinge must arouse suspicion, though it may be that the original hinge has rusted away and the replacement could itself be two centuries old.

7 The colour of the wood should be uneven, but black marks with distinct edges show that the wood was attached to something else and that the chest is made up. Where there are joins or where there is woodwork of any kind, look for unexplained dark areas – it may be a faker's way of trying to cover his traces.

8 The base of the chest should be quite plain and rough, and be grey in colour. If it is not it could be innocent but fatuous refurbishment, or a piece of wood from something else. Always bear in mind that 'old' chests have often been made from old floorboards, which may bear indentations from thousands of pairs of boots. Smooth, unexplained rounded depressions in any piece of old oak, not necessarily just chests, should not be overlooked.

9 Sometimes the cut in the plank side is a 'V', sometimes the cut-out is more elaborate. In this case it is well on the way to a bracket foot. If it is too fancy it may indicate that it is a later amendment.

protected by metal fittings. The handles are usually inset, and there are also carrying handles. Most military chests are made in two parts, for easy handling, and there is often a bureau fitting, adding to the value. Amongst the woods used were padouk, cedar, camphor and, of course, mahogany, and as they were made for hard use veneer was not employed (though it is often used in even good quality reproductions). If elaborate feet are fitted, these are likely to screw off. Although plain and restrained, military chests fetch large sums of money on account of their masculine appeal.

Specimen chests are a bank of small drawers in a slender upright housing. When there is a hinged flap which falls across the drawers to prevent them being opened they are called Wellington chests.

Victorian and Edwardian chests of drawers, for many years disregarded and not worth the trouble of carrying from the auction room, have enjoyed a revival as earlier pieces have risen dramatically in price. They are ideal for 'refashioning', for turning into something else. The plain ones can be painted or otherwise transformed. Because of their simple structure they lend themselves to complete rebuilding, and as in many ways they represent bottom-of-the-range furniture there is less reluctance to subject them to drastic stripping and bleaching. Some of these chests of drawers are made of pitch pine; these do not strip very well.

The best Victorian chests of drawers are superbly made, and the columns at the sides often improve the overall look. If heaviness is the quality required, why not make the most of it with columns? Very few were meaninglessly ornate, as chest of drawers were now regarded as bedroom furniture and were for private use not display. Plain unvarnished oak was often used by Edwardian makers, unadorned and unpretentious; fashionable models had wooden handles and discreet inlays. These are far more attractive than some of the Jacobethan chests of drawers, sometimes on legs with superfluous stretchers (known as Jacobethan because there was confusion as to whether they were in the Jacobean or Elizabethan style). The dressing chest was another item of bedroom furniture, an ordinary small chest of drawers with a swing mirror. There are a few examples with a washstand unit, used as boarding-house furniture.

VI

Clothes Presses and Wardrobes

Until less than ten years ago clothes or linen presses and wardrobes were the ugly ducklings of the antiques trade, and fine Georgian presses veneered with great sheets of flame mahogany had difficulty in making more than two or three hundred pounds. The press was originally a cupboard with drawers to hold books or clothes, and the unwary will often open what they think is a wardrobe and find a tier of large drawers. Many presses have long since been converted, the drawers and their runners taken out, and hooks or a clothes rail fitted. In the past they have been bought mainly for practical use, and as they have been put in bedrooms and are therefore not seen by casual visitors, who thus cannot be impressed, the value of a press or wardrobe has been judged on its efficiency.

Some articles of furniture that look like presses can be cabinets-on-chests, or even a closed-front bookcase. Extra value is added by mouldings, especially top mouldings, cornices, original brass handles and key plates, and the quality of the inlay or applied decoration. Most presses have bracket feet, and some have a carved apron. The press merged gradually into the wardrobe, which could become an intricate bag of tricks, with accommodation for almost every article of clothing or accessory. In the 1930s there was a vogue for the compactum, a wardrobe with a chest of drawers attached at the side, sometimes with a lift-up top on the chest to harbour collar-studs and other exotic treasures of the past.

Many Victorian and Edwardian wardrobes are incredibly large, sometimes 10ft (3m) across, and in the past they were bought just for the sake of the large sheets of veneer that were used on the doors. Most of them are built up in sections, so that they are more easily moved than may at first seem the case. Sheraton-revival wardrobes can be very handsome, though the shell-type pull-out handles on the drawers are less elegant than the brass fitments on the originals. The Art Nouveau-inspired wardrobes in oak with pewter or copper panels, and perhaps inlay of ebony or other woods, are greatly under-rated.

The less said about the commercial wardrobes that were produced after World War I the better. They were often black-stained, plentifully decorated with cock-beading, and frequently had a full-length mirror affixed to the front of the door. The better quality wardrobes had mirrors on the inside of the door. Streamlined wardrobes from the Art Deco period were made in some quantity but there was little even the most adventurous designers could do with the structure. As veneer was cheap, sometimes even the ordinary chain-store wardrobes can be spectacular, with walnut or flame mahogany veneer applied in matching spreads, or in bedazzling blotches. The quieter veneers were often criss-crossed by boxwood diagonal stringing.

The best quality wardrobes in satinwood had painted rococo or milkmaid scenes in neat ovals, though transfers were sometimes used. Lacquer was a 1920s novelty finish; lacquering was a popular do-it-yourself hobby, but some impressive lacquer wardrobes were made with painted scenes in the Japanese fashion. The most agreeable and unassuming are probably the functional Heal-type wardrobes. As more houses are equipped with built-in wardrobes there will always be enough free-standing specimens to supply the demand of the antiques trade.

Even the mediocre wardrobes are worth looking at with a view to transformation. The doors can be taken off, the hinges removed and the betraying wooden cut-out filled in, and they can be converted into bookshelves or with the doors left intact, bookcases. If the finish is awful the wardrobe can be stripped down, even bleached, and turned into something else. It can even be cut down to serve a purpose. The one universal quality about a wardrobe is that it can hold a lot of things. Suitably painted, stencilled, marbled, or given some fantasy finish, it can be the answer to storage problems in playroom, child's bedroom, or wherever.

VII

Corner Cupboards

It is odd that the only kinds of cupboards of any consequence, unless they are seventeenth-century or earlier and bear names such as aumbry or livery cupboard, are corner cupboards. Early hanging corner cupboards were bow-fronted, sometimes in plain wood, or japanned or painted with figurative subjects, often of Dutch inspiration, sometimes crude copies of Dutch paintings. Although the doors tend to warp and twist, bow-fronted cupboards are the most desirable today.

There are cupboards with no upper doors – built-in corner fitments rather than cupboards. Some doors were taken off later; look for signs of missing hinges. Either wood was removed where there were butt hinges or there will be nail holes from missing 'H'-shaped hinges. A carved swag somehow out of character may be disguising some amendment to the original piece.

The hanging corner cupboard was not so suitable for the display of heavy pieces as the free-standing version, and until recently the hanging cupboard has been somewhat

WILLIAM AND MARY WALNUT CHEST ON STAND

1 Although genuine (but acknowledged that restoration has been carried out – exactly what is unspecified) this chest-on-stand looks unwieldy, and the stand looks too weak to stand the weight of the enormous chest, especially as it is in walnut. Often the stand was too weak and there was a steady trade in replacement stands, known as Hackney Road stands from the place where they were made. These replacements are now themselves antique, and it is a matter of shrewd judgement whether the stand matches the chest.

2 A strong stretcher is vital, and it is evident that this is a replacement. Nevertheless this chest-on-stand still managed to make £3,960 at auction.

3 Could it be that the whole piece of furniture is suspect? Certainly there is a good profit in making up such articles. Generally, it is interesting to see if the tops of such chests are veneered. As these were too high to be seen in genuine chests-on-stands there was no point in making much of a show on top and the topmost surfaces were left unveneered. This particular example has a cornice.

4 The apron is rather elaborate, and should be examined to see if everything matches and nothing has been cut down or made good. The centre arch in the apron is not quite level.

5 The figuring on the walnut matches quite well. If there is damage to the veneer it is necessary to provide new veneer which fits in with the existing figuration. If it is decided to replace damaged veneer on one of the drawers, either wholly or in part, the banding round each drawer is a complication.

6 All the drawers should be removed, and as this piece is known to have been restored, they should be taken out together and the carcase examined very carefully to find out exactly what has been done and whether there is renovation which on the surface is not apparent. The drawers of course should be examined individually, making certain that they slide well, and that the linings and the bottoms are intact.

7 The handles are in period, but there is always a chance that they may be reproduction, and this goes too for the escutcheons and the locks. Examine the inside of the drawers for unexplained screw holes or unexpected darkening of the wood. If there is real uncertainty take out one of the screws and see if it is flat-ended. Pointed screws are fairly modern. But this is not decisive: with big money at stake, fakers may well sheer off the points of modern screws and begrime them to make them appear old, though it is still more difficult to disguise the difference between the even thread of machine-made screws, and the uneven thread of the hand-made variety.

8 The drawers of the stand do not appear to be fitting very well. There may be a simple reason for this; or there may be some deep-seated trouble. Inconvenient as it may be, a purchaser should go to the trouble of having the chest taken off the stand for a more detailed inspection.

47

neglected. Even though fine examples with arched broken pediments and good quality inlay were made, it is evident that the good furniture-makers were more interested in the design possibilities of the free-standing cupboard and many of the hanging cupboards are plain affairs made by country craftsmen.

As a piece of furniture the corner cupboard was not valued highly; it was not mentioned by Hepplewhite, Sheraton, or Chippendale. Sometimes cupboards are made to fit into odd shapes, and these may not be right-angled. It is therefore advisable to check this when buying, and also to try to make certain that a free-standing corner cupboard is what it makes out to be and not a low-value but genuine hanging cupboard placed on a made-up base. Some corner cupboards were made with back boards running from top to bottom. If in two parts, they should match. However, if they don't, it doesn't mean to say that the piece is unacceptable. Corner cupboards, by virtue of their location, are prone to damp, and so backs may have been replaced because they are rotten.

Corner cupboards were often painted inside, usually a dull red, but sometimes blue, and it might seem that this detracts from a good piece of furniture. In fact, it sometimes looks the work of some latterday do-it-yourself enthusiast who has decided to brighten up the place.

It is important to decide if wood doors have been replaced by glass, as glass-fronted specimens are worth a good deal more. In eighteenth- and early nineteenth-century work the glazing bars were usually jointed into the frame of the door, and marking lines made with a knife when the glass was put in are sometimes visible. Fakers believe that the ideal number of panes to put in a glazed front is thirteen, and often religiously keep to it. Sometimes, of course, there were thirteen panes in an original front, but not invariably. No faker can reproduce the minor blemishes in old glass with the slight rippling, though it is worth remembering that during World War II when glass was scarce, glass of an inferior quality with the authentic ripple was made, and can still be seen in the windows of older houses. So faulty glass may not be so old as it seems.

The best full-length corner cupboards were architectural in inspiration, designed sometimes in pairs for grand panelled rooms. Pine was often used for high-quality cupboards to match existing room panelling. An attractive feature of open-front cupboards is the rounded barrel back, sometimes given a shell shape, a decorative device which is very impressive and little used on other furniture, probably because there was no place for it to be set.

VIII

Court Cupboards, Dressers and Sideboards

There are certain items that have alternative names, all of which are confusing, and typical of these is the court cupboard. The word 'court' has nothing to do with royalty and is merely the French for 'short', and the 'cup-board' was originally a board for cups, and by extension a side table or sideboard for the display of 'cups' which may also include plates. At these side tables food was also placed for serving, preparing, and dressing – thus the origin of the dresser. Another name for the court cupboard was the

Left: Illustration from a Maple catalogue of 1881, a 'Chippendale' corner bracket.
Right: Illustration from the same catalogue, an 'Early English' corner cabinet, showing the delight in spindles, fondly believed to be characteristics of all 'Early English' furniture.

buffet. Or hall or parlour cupboard. Even this is confusing, for strictly speaking a parlour is a room in a monastery or nunnery where speaking is allowed.

Court cupboards can date from the sixteenth century. There are two kinds; those with an open base and those with a closed base, those with an open base being much more interesting. These are large impressive pieces of furniture, in three tiers, each level connected by sturdy bulbous supports, of melon shape, of the kind favoured by the Victorians and chain-store furniture-makers of the 1930s. Their purpose was as display stands, and with their ornate and often ill-matched carving they set out to impose, and still do, commanding high prices. Many experienced dealers go through life without having had a genuine court cupboard pass through their hands. Court cupboard themes were a source of inspiration to nineteenth-century furniture-makers in oak. There were people with the expertise to carry out the necessary work. *Ackermann's Repository* 1827 testified that: 'We have so many skilful workmen in Gothic that very elaborate pieces of furniture may be made at a moderate price compared with what it was a few years ago.' In the form of a buffet, the court cupboard became nothing more than a food trolley.

The closed-base court cupboard has something of the air of a rather baleful top-heavy sideboard with a superfluous storey. There was usually a profusion of carving, and as many court cupboards had no moulding round the top these were added later. The court cupboard is interesting historically in that, unlike most other pieces of furniture, it led nowhere, though this did not prevent manufacturers of the 1920s and 1930s trying their hand on it, with carving running riot, and the massive melon-shaped supports refined and turned into inconsequential swellings.

The dresser originated from the livery cupboard, where the livery or portion of food for overnight consumption by the master was kept. The steward would fetch food and 'dress' it (prepare it) and serve it. The buffet or sideboard developed as a board on which to dress the food: thus the dresser. The first development was the drawers under the top board, often supported by turned legs, with and without stretchers.

49

An Edwardian mahogany and marquetry commode of high quality sold for £2,200 in 1988. Twenty years ago these were everyday 'trade goods' of little consequence. If there is a fault it is in the mechanical picture-making of the marquetry, lacking sparkle.

Opposite, above: A Regency mahogany bow-front chest of about 1810. This was bedroom furniture so decoration was kept to a minimum. Useful, functional and worth around £1,000.
Below: It is interesting to compare this chest of about 1710 with the Regency example in the previous illustration. This one is rather more valuable with its walnut marquetry which, however, has been restored. The bracket feet look genuine but they are actually later additions.

Topless dressers continued, some very sophisticated with cabriole legs and elaborate scrolled friezes. The space beneath the drawers was enclosed, and about 1700 there came a superstructure of shelves. Whereas most 'country' furniture derived from London models, the dresser really was evolved, developed, and brought to a high level of structural intricacy in the country. Mostly they are of oak (especially) and pine, but many other woods such as ash, elm, and chestnut were used.

Certain regions concentrated on certain features, and Montgomery in Wales was acknowledged as the producer of very high-quality pieces. Fashions came and went without apparent reason. Cupboards in the superstructure of Welsh dressers disappeared, but remained across the border in Shropshire, and in Lancashire and the North. The cabriole leg apparently never appeared in Wales (perhaps regarded as too typical of the detested English), but it did in Shropshire.

The pine dresser has for long been the quintessential kitchen showpiece for those who do not go in for laid-out fitted kitchens. It seems to have been a Welsh type, with open shelves until about 1840. Dating pine dressers is very difficult, and it is a brave man who would state that a specific specimen belonged to the eighteenth century. Sometimes it is not easy to tell whether a pine dresser is genuine or made-up, though the presence of orange-box lids is, to say the least of it, a guide. The Welsh pine dressers of the 1840s and 1850s are magnificent. And these were made in a country where the total population at the time was no more than a million.

The sideboard is related in usage to the cumbersome court cupboard and the functional dresser, and for the last forty years of the eighteenth century was arguably one of the most elegant pieces of furniture then in use. The classic sideboard was in mahogany, with or without inlay, often with shell motifs and stringing. It could be straight-fronted, bow, or serpentine; the more ornate the shape the more valuable. The legs were usually six in number, of tapering square section with spade feet, in two groups of three. There were three sections; the centre was a drawer over the knee-hole; the outer sections were cupboards, later becoming drawers.

In the Regency period the outer sections were extended downwards, fitted with squat, turned or ornamental feet, and the result was a heavier more formidable piece of furniture. Ornamental columns were often added. The trend was for sideboards to become solid-doored cabinets, and the flattened-arch design of the 1840s held sway for half a century – despite the gargantuan exhibition sideboards with heavy, useless top pieces and a profusion of brilliant carving (often incorporating studies of dead birds and/or Shakespearean characters).

Sideboards could be fitted with back rails or galleries, and as the nineteenth century progressed it became difficult to distinguish between sideboards and cabinets, especially when they were named 'chiffoniers' and 'credenzas'. Many so-called chiffoniers are small sideboards with the top rail or back removed and a new shelf added.

So everything is not what it seems, and when credenzas and chiffoniers were top favourites for overseas importers there was no reluctance to convert a humble sideboard into a more desirable object. However, as credenzas are by and large so enormously ornate it needed a good deal of imagination to see a possibility in a sideboard, transmogrify it as one might.

The Edwardians made some elegant sideboards in the Georgian manner, with good inlay and the use of satinwood, and these have had sufficient wear to cause some uncertainty amongst laymen and some non-specialist dealers as to whether they are genuine Georgian pieces. They also made what might be the popular sideboard par excellence – big, chunky, needing six men to move it and indestructible if not wanted. Its main features: a large mirror in the back; pillars supporting a pediment; panelled doors.

Rather more fetching are the curious sideboards made from the 1890s onwards which reflected Art Nouveau motifs, inlay, flower designs, heavy hinges, pewter and iron fittings, bronze panels, heart-shaped cut-outs, and odd flat top-knots, as if something was going to be added and the designer had not made a decision before the piece was sold. Often in oak, sometimes stained green, these sideboards were the most commercially suitable means of bringing Art Nouveau to the masses. They are greatly under-valued. If you see one, look at the construction; there is often pegging that would do a master-joiner proud.

The 1920s saw some dismal sideboards, often dark-stained with barley-twist legs and thin bobbin-moulding round the doors. Many are known as Jacobethan, because there was some confusion as to whether they were in the Jacobean or Elizabethan style. Of course they are in neither. But many of the 1930s sideboards, sometimes bow-fronted using bentwood techniques on the plywood and veneered in high-grade burr walnut and other expensive woods, deserve appreciation of craftsmanship. The interiors are often very fine, with good finishing and attention to detail. The best of these were designed by named craftsmen, and it is always worthwhile looking for a manufacturer's name-plate, often inside one of the doors or drawers, or on the back. With their stream-lined design they are ideal not only for immediate use but for transformation purposes; there is a wide disparity between the prices obtained in London, where they are recognised for what they are, and in the provinces.

And then there are the severely geometric and functional sideboards. They are the descendants of the Morris chair, destined for sensible no-nonsense folk with limited room available, so such sideboards were small. Design was basic, and there were no supernumerary shelves for oddments.

IX

Desks and Bureaux

Any table could be used to write on, and what are termed 'library tables' or 'writing tables' may have been used for some other purpose entirely. There is, however, no ambiguity about the best-known form of desk, the bureau, which led eventually to the roll-top and its American big brother the Wells Fargo with its vast number of pigeon-holes.

The first writing furniture was a box with a sloping lid, sometimes confused with a Bible box, but this was not a very convenient solution and it was better to have the box containing all the impedimenta on a stand. The flap of the greatly improved box came over and formed a writing surface. This could be supported by overlapping the base, by pull-out slides, or by an arrangement similar to a gateleg table, with the centre gate opening and supporting the flap.

It was soon realised that the space beneath the desk could be utilised, and it was

These French display cabinets of about 1910 parallel in many ways Edwardian reproduction furniture made in England at the same time. There is a flaw in taste – the short legs seem out of proportion, but they serve as corner furniture, always a desirable asset, so the £4,000 they command is realistic.

Opposite, above: English or French? The buhl (tortoise shell and brass) facings and the rich gilt mountings on this encoignure tend to suggest that the piece was actually made in France. An admirable corner piece, and of sufficient quality for ebonising.
Below: This press cupboard or court cupboard bears an uncanny likeness to the mule chest illustrated earlier on page 42. Both purport to be Elizabethan, both have been meddled with. They have not been distressed.

provided with drawers. The fall of early bureaux was narrow; later the angle was increased. Bureaux were prestige pieces, and the fitted interiors could be marvels of craftsmanship, with secret drawers, elegant stepping, and exquisite detail, as in the provision of pillars for the centre section of the interior. Because of the great demand for bureaux a good deal of tampering has taken place over the years, and they have sometimes been revived too much. Walnut should have different shades of colour; some restorers clean off to a single light brown shade. Sometimes bracket feet were substituted for bun feet; move the larger bottom drawer to find holes where original bun feet were fitted. Drop handles were replaced; look for two sets of round holes with a mark in the middle. The Victorians fitted knobs, irrespective of the anachronism. There are usually signs of this. Sometimes plain bureaux were veneered with thin walnut from Victorian loo tables.

Did the bureau have a top on? Look for holes which may outline the story. Virginian walnut was imported from the 1720s onwards, so larger sections of wood were available. Burr walnut was expensive, and sides and backs were often left unveneered, or straight-grained walnut was used. So what might appear to be a faulty piece of furniture could be absolutely genuine. Sometimes a crack has appeared where the carcase has shifted through changes of temperature beneath the veneer.

The designs and woods used in bureaux conformed to fashion – oak, walnut, mahogany – but of course exotic woods were used for extra-special pieces and the country maker naturally used country woods. The tell-tale sign of a country piece is the simple interior, often very basic with a bank of drawers beneath pigeon-holes in the form of uncluttered arches. Architect-inspired bureaux, such as those influenced by William Kent (1684–1748), could be massive creations, well over 5ft (1.5m) wide. Generally speaking, the smaller the bureau the better, so that they can fit snugly into the modern home. Original brass fittings and interiors are a decided plus.

If the bureau is a valuable piece of furniture, what can be said about the bureau bookcase? Twenty years ago the average dealer had bought and sold several, and they were known affectionately as 'BBs'. Today, unless they are exceptionally crude or reproduction, they are out of his range. The fittings of the upper section varied enormously, and the bookcase section could be mirrored, glazed, or panelled. Sometimes side drawers supported the fall front. Some bureau bookcases are fitted with carrying handles, on both sections. Tops can be seen to be top-heavy; occasionally the typical broken pediment is overpowering and the buyer must judge whether this is a feature of the design or whether a marriage has taken place and the top has nothing to do with the bottom. Sometimes a plain top has had a pediment supplied for it (provincial makers often made fairly low bureau bookcases because their customers lived in homes where the ceilings were low).

The bureau bookcase went into decline in the mid-nineteenth century but the Edwardians revived the conception, reproducing with a good deal of skill eighteenth-century examples and evolving their own oak equivalents, often with Art Nouveau motifs. These were basic, with the bureau interiors hardly more than a succession of equal-shaped pigeon-holes with a couple of token drawers. The bookcase section was sometimes open, sometimes glazed with leaded lights, or stained glass, or half and half. Cupboards were sometimes placed in the bookcase section, apparently at random, an annoyance to any book-lover, a species that never has enough orthodox shelf room. The fall-fronts of the bureau were normally kept up by slides, but an alternative was a

An eighteenth-century walnut bureau of a very basic type, but because it was uncluttered and not improved it sold for £6,200. Sometimes it is not worthwhile to smarten furniture up.

metal rod sliding under the interior of the bureau and holding the front horizontal.

Jacobethan bureau bookcases, or even bookcases, in stained oak with leaded lights, are much in demand in Germany, but with their applied stuck-on ornament and cheap fitments, their geometrical mouldings on the drawers to imitate panels, they have little to commend them except solidity of carcase construction.

An alternative to the fall-front mechanism of the bureau was the sliding cylinder, known as the tambour. These cylinders could be solid or formed from connected fillets of wood. Structurally, the cylinder bureau was more complicated (for the cylinder when rolled back has to go somewhere) and consequently it was a top-of-the-market product. It was actually less useful, as naturally the cylinder could not provide a writing surface as the fall-front flap did (though whether it was used for much writing is open to question). The cylinder bureau was provided with an upper storey on occasions.

A very thin line separates bureaux and bureau bookcases from other pieces such as secretaires, scrutoires, escritoires, etc: all alternative names for writing furniture, culled from old papers and taken up with enthusiasm by auctioneers' cataloguers. Sometimes the piece of furniture is a chest-on-chest with a writing unit sandwiched in between. It would need someone 9ft (2.7m) tall to get at the top drawers of the upper chest. So why make it? Who knows? Far more elegant is the secretaire chest, a writing unit atop a quite orthodox chest. As for the distinction between a secretaire bookcase and a bureau bookcase, the difference mainly lies in the slope of the bureau top. Both serve exactly the same purpose.

The pedestal desk was not subject to the vagaries of fashion. It was a decidedly masculine piece of furniture, with plenty of useful drawers in the pedestals and in the desk unit. Large pedestal desks with drawers both sides are known as partners' desks. Variation was provided with kidney-shaped tops and rounded pedestals. Sometimes there was a leather inset in the top, and all things considered these have lasted well, and if not are easily renovated or replaced. Mostly the pedestals rested directly on the floor without feet.

If the pedestal desk is masculine, the bonheur-du-jour is feminine, often simperingly so. It is a small elegant writing table, usually with drawers, with sections at the back of the writing surface. These units can include drawers, pigeon-holes, cupboards, or even a mirror, in various permutations, but except for a few sturdy Regency specimens they look as though a well-directed kick would dismantle them. It was a type of furniture much reproduced by the Edwardians in their favourite woods, mahogany and satinwood.

One of the most popular articles of small furniture, and akin to the bonheur-du-jour in that the writing surface is pathetic, is the Davenport desk. Captain Davenport ordered a desk from the important firm of Gillow in the 1790s. They were 'very useful articles for industrious young ladies' declared J. C. Loudon in his *Encyclopaedia of Cottage, Farm and Villa Architecture* in 1833. The early examples (and there are forty-five distinct designs) were no more than small chests of drawers with desk compartments on top. The classic Davenport had four drawers on the side, with dummies on the other. Earlier types had the sloping desk compartment on slides to

George IV mahogany library desk of about 1825, very desirable as study and office furniture. This desk is double sided and may be termed a partners' desk.

This splendid Carlton House desk dates from the early years of this century, and was sold for £8,200, an excellent price for what is, if not exactly a reproduction, at least a recreation. The original Carlton House desks appeared in pattern books of 1788.

accommodate the knees. By the 1850s the sliding top was often replaced by a fixed top. There was often a brass or wooden gallery, and as this became a quintessential Victorian article a firescreen was sometimes incorporated, and gadgetry, such as secret drawers and pop-up sections, was eagerly welcomed. Some Davenports had a tiny drawer to hold the ink-bottle. Davenports were usually flush with the floor or provided with bun feet or similar truncated supports, with or without castors. The jutting-out top was supported by a pair of legs, ornate cabriole, turned, fluted, or column, or in mid-Victorian combination, fixed on a narrow platform.

Many desks were made for commercial purposes, of a type familiar to those who watch television adaptations of Dickens – high, often with a lift-up lid, at which clerks sat on high schools. They receive little attention in the sale rooms, and occupy the same position as country chairs, but they are ideal for those who are looking for a useful piece of antique furniture at no great cost. Children's desks are always popular: reasonably priced, not particularly distinctive, but often rugged and well-made if Victorian; if later, ghastly and a waste of money.

X

Mirrors

There are all kinds of mirrors. Of all the multitude of objects an antique dealer buys and sells each year, the large mirrors cause him the most trepidation, as not so many years ago monster mirrors could not be given away, whatever the quality of the frame – and in many eighteenth-century mirrors the frames have a magnificence and bravura it is difficult to find in any other furniture of the period. The most common mirror is the toilet mirror, still about in large quantities at very modest prices. These were introduced to Britain from Holland in the Queen Anne period, and there is a good deal of variety considering the limitations – a mirror on a base which may contain drawers. The mirrors themselves can be almost any shape, a serpentine top being one of the more desirable. In early examples, the base could consist of a tiny bureau. Bevelled glass is a plus, and so is the original glass, which was thinner than modern replacement glass. To discern the thickness of mirror glass hold a finger or thumb nail against the mirrored surface; if the reflection is close, it is thin glass.

In antique mirrors a degree of spotting or missing silvering is moderately acceptable, but in Victorian toilet mirrors not so. Silvering may not be a job that demands massive qualifications, but it is very hard to find someone to do it. The bases of eighteenth-century mirrors can be exquisitely finished with inlay and banding, and ivory keyplates and draw-pulls can add to the effect. Bases are often finished off with small bun or bracket feet. The most vulnerable parts of a toilet mirror are the knobs and finials where the mirror swings, and these are often replaced, sometimes with parts that don't match, for toilet mirrors are sold for use and if they don't tilt temporary repairs are carried out which don't get properly done.

The three major categories of looking glasses are pier glasses, overmantel mirrors, and wall mirrors. The pier glass was hung on the pier wall; that is, the wall between the tall eighteenth-century windows of the grand houses of the nobility. These could be 7ft (2.13m) or 8ft (2.44m) in height; in the ordinary middle-class home they were no more than 4ft (1.22m) high. For mirror glass was fiendishly expensive, and for really long glasses the mirror was in two pieces. Frames were wide, for the same reason – to make the mirrors appear bigger without increasing the area of the glass – and additional height was added by cresting.

In the late seventeenth century frames were veneered with crossbanding in various woods, a favourite being olive and walnut. Marquetry and lacquer were often used, but the material that turned the mirror into something magnificent was gesso (plaster and glue size), suitably gilded. The cresting was extravagant, with shells, plumes, and, much used in concave circular mirrors, the eagle. Some mirrors were equipped with candle sconces. Gesso declined, and carved wood and gilt became fashionable. One of the reasons was perhaps the inherent fragility of gesso, easily broken off into chalky fragments and susceptible to damp. If you have some old gilt picture frames stored in a cellar, they are likely to be decorated with gesso, and after a few months they may as well be thrown away.

Some of the most delightful eighteenth-century mirrors are the plain mahogany ones with fretwork cresting and apron (much reproduced by the Edwardians). The

QUEEN ANNE
WALNUT BUREAU

1 Check that all the drawers are in order by taking them all out, examining the bottoms and the linings (sides), checking for worm not only in the drawers but in the interior of the structure. If one of the drawers won't open it may be (a) because it is locked (b) something is in the drawer which is jamming it, or (c) the structure has warped. It may be possible to clear a stuck drawer from inside, unless it is the top one. In a high-quality piece of furniture such as this it would be inadvisable to try to get at a drawer by taking the back off. If a drawer is locked – and it is a long drawer – it is possible in some pieces of furniture to prise up the structure above the drawer, and so release the tongue, but not here, for the walnut is too vulnerable.

2 The bracket feet are obviously genuine in this bureau, but where there is doubt turn the piece of furniture on its side and examine the underneath, looking for superfluous screw holes or discoloured areas of wood which may indicate that the feet are not original. You will probably find that there are blocks to add strength to the structure, but these are not suspicious. Some bureaux have had their bracket feet replaced by bun feet in the Victorian period, not only because these were more fashionable but because the bracket feet may have been worn.

3 The walnut veneer may be damaged, and sometimes it is more difficult to match plain veneer than the more exotic variety with its whirls and extravagant figuring.

4 Check that the crossbanding is undamaged and complete, and decide, if there is damage, whether it is an easy job to repair or replace. Crossbanding often comes out in little oblongs, and if the base wood is cleaned a suitable piece can be slotted in without great effort.

5 The slides which support the fall-front of the bureau should be reasonably free from wobble, though if there is looseness it is easily put right by adding on a sliver of wood to the slide, gluing being sufficient as any pressure will help rather than hinder.

6 As at some time in the past the fall-front will have inevitably been lowered without pulling out the supporting slides, the hinges may be slack, needing to be rescrewed or reset.

7 Inside the bureau top, the pigeon-holes and drawers should be complete, and any accessories, such as knobs to the tiny drawers, should be consistent. It is likely that the writing surface will be ink-stained. If the stain has faded it may be wiser to leave well alone as an interesting period feature, but ink-stains can be removed with oxalic acid or household bleach.

8 Handles and all metal accessories should be in period, and the drop-handles on this 1710 bureau of course are. If too bright and shiny there is a possibility of them being recently affixed reproductions, and the only alternative to replacing them with the real thing, at great cost, is to tone down the metal.

---

most impressive are the great architectural set-pieces. The most outlandish are the Chinese-style and rococo asymmetrical mirrors; this was an area in which the French influence was dominant. Long before it became popular in the average home for small tables, trays, and boxes, papier-mâché was used for frames, gilded and burnished.

In the last forty years of the eighteenth century the Neoclassical movement provided mirrors with swags of husks, vases, paterae, honeysuckles, rams' heads, ox skulls, and sphinxes. This ornamentation was applied in composition and not wood, threaded on wire, and thus not very long-lived. The Victorians liked florid mirrors, and girandoles, incorporating candleholders, were very popular and produced in many variations. Very often the Victorians regilded earlier frames, and these often show a speckled effect.

A Victorian bird's-eye maple Davenport c1850 with all the desirable features including a rising rear section, ample pigeon holes and drawers. The definitive ladies' desks, they were made in vast quantities. Their rise in value is incredible, as much as eighty times in twenty years.

Overmantels, making a room seem much larger, could be overpowering, and a much produced form consisted of three horizontal plates of glass, a frieze with classical figures, surmounted by a cornice with gilt balls and tassels. Tassels were popular amongst the mirror-makers. Overmantels were often in ebonised wood with gold painted decoration, with and without pillars. Some of the cheaper overmantels were made in softwood and stained to imitate mahogany.

Cheval mirrors are long mirrors, hinged in the middle, and set on a base consisting of a stretcher connected to two pairs of wide-spaced legs. In some examples there is a unit containing small drawers between the pairs of legs. The cheval mirror could be equipped with candleholders. Mentioned by Sheraton in 1793, cheval mirrors were invented when large sheets of glass were cheap and easily obtainable. The supporting uprights of the cheval mirror could be turned, square-section, plain or fluted, barley-twist, or, in Victorian examples, richly carved in walnut, rosewood, or other expensive woods. Some cheval mirrors being sold today are not what they seem, but the full-length mirrors of wardrobes put into an easily assembled structure.

Above: A George I giltwood and gesso mirror with swan-neck pediment. Notice that there is some damage to the gesso ornament, and wisely no-one has attempted to put it right. There is a time to restore and a time to leave well alone.
Opposite: A magnificent painted rococo mirror. Twenty years ago this was in a small Sussex antique shop at less than £100 pounds; dealers fought shy of it because of its size and vulnerability.

Left: Continental, possibly Spanish, mirror of about 1750.
Right: An English mirror of the same period. Is there anything that makes this one particularly English?

Detail of the cresting on a classic eighteenth-century mirror, plain mahogany with simple inlay and no gesso to get damaged.

The name (French for horse) is curious, and there are various theories. The least likely is because there is a base consisting of four feet (but we don't have a cheval table or a cheval chest of drawers); then it could be named after the frame (the same naming mechanism occurs in clothes horses); there is also an old speculation that it is derived from 'a pulley or horse that was part of the mechanism for moving the glass in some examples'. What mechanism? A cheval glass is usually tilted with the hands. For those who were confused by the name there were alternative titles, such as a screen dressing glass, or Psyche, though that was not much more explicit. It is only recently that cheval glasses have been sought after. Their legs have been used to make sofa tables or coffee tables in the not-too-distant past.

Many different shapes of wall mirror were produced in the 1920s and 1930s. An elongated octagonal shape was one of the most popular, usually with an oak surround. The glass was often bevelled and of high quality, and this was especially true of the Art Deco mirrors, in which a heavy frame was replaced by chrome strip, sometimes with added ornament. A happy revival was that of the round convex mirror of the eighteenth century, made now in composition, as well as gilt wood. You may see gilt-framed mirrors of uncertain age in curiously large quantities; these are the latest gimmicks, consisting of mirror glass (very cheap) in gilt picture frames.

XI

Screens

Except for screens used as room separators, the two major groups are pole and cheval. The pole screen followed furniture fashions, and the decoration on the screens, which slid up and down the pole, with a swivel facility, or hung from a cross-piece, reflected popular taste amongst the middle classes who were the main customers for the pole screen, a genteel device to protect sensitive skins from the heat of a fire. The rich were a hardier breed. The bases often mirror the designs of tripod tables or small tables with platform bases.

Much of the value of a pole screen lies in the screen itself and what is on it. Original needlework is a plus; earlier needleworkers employed small stitches, those who came later larger ones, and pole screens were ideal showplaces for fashionable Berlin woolwork. In the eighteenth century, flowers, fruit, and leaves were most popular, followed by a brief excursion into neo-classical subjects.

The cheval screen was put in front of an empty grate, and, to say the least of it, was a good deal more decorative than the copper or grille firescreens which came later and are the staple stock of antiques dealers in a small way of business. The wrought-iron firescreens can, however, be of good quality, and even if rusty, renovate well without much trouble.

Cheval screens were usually on two pairs of feet, sometimes with a turned stretcher, and the frame of the picture, often needlework of some kind, good, bad, and indifferent, was usually ornate. For many, the cheval screen was, in fact, a picture on a stand. Some cheval screens had a writing slope which folded flush against the picture. It seems an odd place to jot down notes or write up one's diary. In the 1920s and 1930s

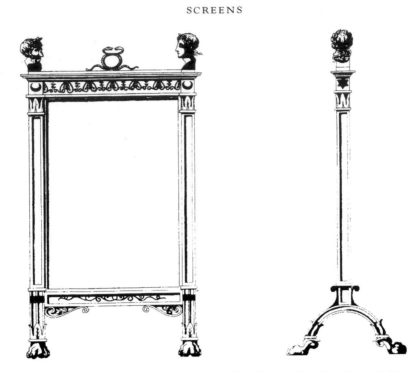

This design for a 'drawing room cheval screen' appeared in George Smith's influential **Designs for Household Furniture** (1808). The chosen medium was not, as might appear, metal, but mahogany.

the screens were often made of wood, usually oak, with a stuck-on plywood plaque depicting galleons or milkmaids, though the traditional screen with a needlework picture was still popular.

Divided full-length screens depend for their value on whatever is painted, stuck, or worked on the various sections. Tooled leather screens were a few years ago worth very little, but they are now appreciating. Lacquer screens were very popular, though usually they show signs of wear. They were a favourite import from Japan in the aesthetic 1870s. Sometimes the decoration of imported Japanese screens consists of ivory cut-outs on a lacquer background, and if badly damaged they are not easy to restore.

Many famous artists painted screens, and these are as good as and as valuable as easel pictures. At the other end of the scale, the screen was the ideal site to decorate with scraps, and this has become a popular present-day pastime, and certainly preferable to pinning posters on walls. Prices of ordinary screens are ridiculously low, odd considering that they are a very useful piece of furnishing equipment and can transform a room.

XII

Stands

The dictionary definition of a stand is quite explicit: 'a base or structure for setting things on; a piece of furniture for hanging things from.' Characteristic of the second group is the much-abused hall stand, with a repository for umbrellas over a tray to hold the drips, a number of coat hooks, usually a mirror and often a drawer to hold gloves or brushes. As it was designed for such diverse purposes, the structure and overall appearance of the hall stand tends to be ungainly, with it looking rather too tall for its width. It was essentially a middle-class piece of furniture; the rich had servants to take away the top clothes of visitors. For those anxious to impress, the hall stand was a massive piece of furniture and could be taken for a sideboard except for the hooks and umbrella receptacle. But most are spindly, and when in bamboo or simulated bamboo are rather mean. Sometimes there are metal panels and scratch carving to add style. Far more saleable are the 'branch' hall stands, with curly wooden pieces springing from the top of an upright, still made in large numbers.

Just because the rectangular hall stands are cheap it doesn't mean to say that they are bargains. They are cheap because they are not in demand, though there is a modest trade in them in the lower echelons of the antiques trade.

Eighteenth-century stands go by various names. The torchère was originally a tall ornamental candlestick or a lampstand, and was presented in many forms, with a single column and small round top on a tripod, or on three long legs terminating in a platform. The top often had a brass gallery and could be rotated. As with urn stands, shorter and more elegant, with the legs projecting from beneath the rimmed platform and sometimes connected by a stretcher, these are now mostly used as plant stands.

The dumb waiter can be classified as either a stand or a three-tiered tripod table, and was defined by Sheraton as 'a useful piece of furniture to serve in some respects the place of a waiter, whence it is so named'. Although they were known earlier, most dumb waiters date from the 1750s, are mostly in mahogany though Regency ones can be in rosewood, and later ones can have a brass gallery. The three circular stages are graduated in size, and are often lipped, and if they are in any way different in style the piece has been made up. Although dumb waiters were sometimes made with only two stages these are not common.

The whatnot or omnium is a spindly piece of furniture with shelves dating from about 1800. The early ones are elegant and modest, with agreeable turned uprights. Sometimes a drawer is incorporated in the design, adding to the value. Most of the whatnots seen today are Victorian, often very ornate with fretted decoration and finials at every point, which are apt to break off or get lost. There are often fiddly friezes to the shelves, also inclined to get damaged. Because whatnots are so vulnerable, a stage may be missing (often there are four including the top), and they should be examined carefully to see if they are intact. Victorian whatnots were usually made in the 'show' woods such as burr walnut. The early whatnots often have castors.

The étagère is an ornamental stand of shelves, in form rather like a superior tea-trolley without wheels, and was a French-influenced piece of furniture. It enjoyed a certain popularity in the late nineteenth century, when there was always a demand for something to put objects on, no matter what. The jardinière is a plant stand. The name is sometimes given, wrongly, to the actual flower pot. There was often a gallery halfway down which served no purpose except to act as support to the legs; the flower pots and their contents could be very heavy. This feature was taken over in the Edwardian plant stand, a familiar open rectangular oak structure comprising four long square-section legs, a top, a carved apron sometimes with fretwork, and a gallery, sometimes with railings. These plant stands were sometimes termed palm stands for no very clear reason save that of swank. The mahogany ones can be elegant, but many of the oak examples are unimpressive and are still very cheap indeed. They are worth considering for transformation purposes, for their cost today is no more than that of the wood if bought new.

Simple pedestals, turned, fluted, or angular, usually on a chunky square platform, are far more attactive, and because of their appeal and saleability have been converted from the uprights of four-posters when four-posters were not wanted, or from other suitable turned furniture members. Among the most expensive stands are the eighteenth-century blackamoor stands and torchères, sometimes converted to electricity. Many of these are ascribed to Venice, where Moors were apparently by no means unknown. Blackamoor stands are a historical curiosity, comparable with the Red Indian full-length figures used in America to advertise tobacconists, or stuffed animals, such as bears, converted into hall stands. And parts of animals, such as stag antlers, often serve the same purpose. These novelties always fetch more in auction than one would think. Whether they can be considered a kind of organic furniture is a matter for debate!

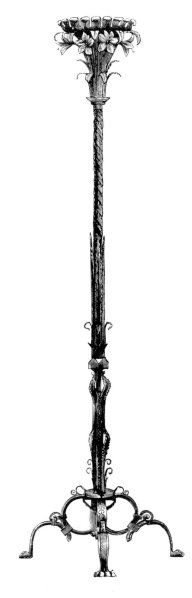

An iron plant stand of 1862.

Two genuine pieces of old oak. At one time pre-eighteenth-century stools were disregarded as of no account, but with more substantial pieces being snapped up these simple articles have come into their own.

XIII

Stools

Many early stools are known as joyned or joynt; this is because they were made by joiners, for even then workers in wood were differentiated. Unless you were fairly important there wasn't much to sit on except stools and benches, or perhaps you perched uncomfortably on a chest. Long neglected, four-legged seventeenth-century stools are now much in demand, and because they look simple to make, fakers have gone into the stool market in a big way. Large numbers of imitations – not necessarily deliberate fakes – were made early in the present century and in the oak boom of the 1920s, and many of them have had sufficient use to make dating of them sometimes difficult, unless they have hinged lids to give access to a small compartment beneath the seat.

Originals were sawn with a hand saw (giving straight marks) not the power-operated circular saw (slightly rounded marks on thick cuts). Look for sharp edges, indicating lack of usage, and any wear should be where it is expected, not chamfered down to create an effect. Signs of decay are welcome, and where the top has been pegged down so that it cannot move easily, contraction of wood, which is inevitable, will split the top. The colour should be uneven. Avoid overall colour particularly if there is a greenish chemical tinge or the patination is dead.

Early carving is not necessarily crude. Crudity could be Victorian faking. Flushed

71

with self-confidence and illusions of grandeur, the fakers imagined that they knew better than the original makers what was in period. Look for holes that cannot be accounted for, a sure sign that a stool has been made up from something else. Equally, black marks with distinct edges show that the wood was attached to something else. Such stools may be made from floor boards or table tops.

There should be dark areas on the polished side, and the grain of the wood should always be visible. Fakers blacken areas where there are joins, to try to disguise any slipshod or anachronistic work. A thin dark area is acceptable, but not several square inches. Look how the wood is cut. Early oak was riven, split with a wedge hammered into the end of the trunk. Thus the grain was torn apart. It was then evened up roughly with plane or adze. The joints rebates will not fit perfectly.

Stools would have been stored sideways, seats outermost, under tables. Sometimes they are called coffin stools, the main reason being a comment by Pepys referring to his 'uncle's corpse in a coffin standing upon joint stools in the chimney in the hall'.

A large number of very crude plank stools were made, often in pine, with plank sides with a 'V' cut in them to give a vaguely four-legged form. These are almost impossible to date, as are the three-legged 'milkmaids' stools' with the legs slotted into round holes in the circular, sometimes octagonal, seat. These are often badly afflicted with woodworm, which helps to give the illusion of age, and it is not unknown for them to be deliberately made from woodwormy planks. Sometimes the legs penetrate above the seat, kept in position by nails driving down the top of the leg, thus causing the wood to expand and fit tightly.

As chairs became more plentiful, and even the common people were allowed to sit on them, the stool was used for other, usually occasional, purposes, and unless they were made for a specific purpose – such as the Victorian piano stools – they followed the designs of chairs. Stools were gilded or painted, and upholstered to match sets of chairs. After the Restoration stools were constructed like chairs, with elaborate carving of legs and stretchers, usually (unlike chairs) all four legs. Beware of chairs which have been cut down to make stools. Stools were covered with velvet, needlework, carpetry, with braids and tasselled fringes of silk, with wool or metal threads around edges.

'X' shape stretchers were typical of William and Mary designs, often very elaborate with highly ornamental finials and exotic legs, often knobbly and tortuous, indicating that the stool had emerged from a plebeian past into something special. Caning was much used in stools, and some had an 'H'-shaped understretcher, though this design feature is quite rare.

Most stools were free standing but some were intended to be placed against the wall. Eighteenth-century stools of the period in mahogany are often plain, sometimes with drop-in seats, with square-section legs. Among the most desirable are the mid eighteenth-century stools in the Gothic style with intricate pierced legs, and friezes in the form of tiny arches. The value of such a stool could be £8,000 or more.

In the late eighteenth century window stools with curved ends appeared, wider than earlier stools, decorated at the front. Some had three legs at front, two at back. Conversation and dressing stools were listed in a trade label of a St Columb cabinet-maker and upholsterer of Cornwall, giving some idea of provincial taste at the time.

The Victorians popularised all manner of stools, though the age's most distinctive example is the tripod piano stool in most woods, the highest quality being in walnut

A Regency mahogany 'X'-frame stool of about 1815 with a cane seat.

and rosewood. These were fitted with massive wind-up mechanisms that are virtually indestructible. Many of the seats were upholstered in leather and buttoned, and if the leather is brittle but otherwise in good condition it should be treated with leather dressing rather than replaced, as the task of buttoning leather is major. Some of the Victorian stools are rather unfortunate, looking like chairs that for some reason have lost their backs. Many were made in the French style, with scroll designs and cabriole legs, sometimes gilded. These were made without much alteration well into the 1920s.

'Useful and artistic furniture' of the 1890s. Perhaps of most interest here is the 'Hamlet' stool, very similar in shape to the 'Thebes' stool sold by Liberty's.

The Victorians also popularised footstools, some of these being known as gout stools, after one of the fashionable diseases of the rich. These were round, oval, rectangular, and square, and lent themselves to upholstering in velvet, beadwork, and Berlin woolwork, and they were often tricked out with braids and tasselled fringes. As these seats were of an uncomplicated shape, such stools lent themselves to amateur upholstering of all kinds. The making of stools was apparently a very popular do-it-yourself activity among amateur carpenters, and impressive and intricate embroidery was often lavished on structures that are hardly more than badly constructed frames.

Among the most distinctive developments in stool design was Liberty's Thebes stool, registered in 1884 and one of the first products of the furnishing and decorating studio, established in 1883. These had thonged leather seats, and were mostly in walnut, but also in mahogany and oak. By the end of the century most of the permutations had been and gone and only in the 1930s was there any sense of adventure, with the functional stools in chrome and other modern metals, from which the ubiquitous bar stool developed.

XIV

Tables

The main early table was of the trestle type, quite narrow, sometimes 25ft (7.5m) long, dismantled when not in use. The diners sat on long benches. The trestle table developed into the refectory table, a name given by the Victorians. Early refectory tables had bulbous legs and massive construction, with floor-level stretchers. The tops were planks – the fewer the better. Widely faked and made-up, refectory tables should be regarded with suspicion. The stretchers should have a good deal of wear where generations of feet have rested on them, and they should be flush with the legs, not inset. One of the best clues is the state of the base of the legs. They should be bruised, maybe chamfered by wear, and where they have rubbed against the floor they should betray this with ingrained dirt and a degree of water damage.

Small tables with fixed tops were used in the private rooms. In the sixteenth century the 'framed' table was introduced. Heavy turned legs are set into a framing at the corners. The draw-top table, with leaves that could be put in and out, was a useful innovation and this was followed in due course by the gateleg table. All these table types have proved their worth, and are made to this day, so it is not surprising that fairly modern gateleg tables can be confused with earlier ones.

So if there is doubt, look for holes for which there doesn't seem to be a reason. Oak gives out tannic acid which slowly erodes iron so where old screws were removed there will be a browny-black discolouration. A hole might mean that once there was a peg, and that the table-top may have belonged to another piece of furniture altogether and the gateleg table being presented as an antique is made up from old wood. If there is a plug rather than a mysterious hole, this also seems to indicate (though not to prove – it may be a fault in the wood itself) that the furniture is not what it purports to be.

The underside should never be stained, nor should it be black. A table is convincing if the underside is light-coloured and dry, sometimes silvery in sheen, old looking and

George III satinwood and rosewood 'D'-shaped card table of about 1800 with ebonised stringing.

A George IV Wilkinson patent concertina action dining table of about 1820, designed to solve the problem of expanding a table without having too much trouble with intrusive legs.

TABLES

raw. Marks of old hinges may be all right, for wrought iron is not strong, and as in early gateleg tables there were heavy flaps to add pressure on hinge joints, replacement hinges may have been fitted a very long time ago.

The value of a gateleg table depends partly on how many people it can seat, for unlike some oversized antiques considerable sums of money are paid for large tables for strenuous family use. Square-ended gateleg tables are less desirable than round or oval, and some have been shaped to conform to fashion, often making the proportions odd, though the arrangement of the stretchers and gates on even top-quality tables can look strange at times, even when they are absolutely authentic. If there are too many planks making up the top it is either a second-quality country-made piece or the table has been made up, maybe using floorboards.

In the eighteenth century the mechanism of the gate was beautified, and as mahogany was stronger the need for stretchers was no longer there. Sometimes the opening-up section is snuggled so close to the basic frame that it is difficult to see at first, harking back to 1620s tables, where the heavily turned legs split down the middle to become the gates; (some of these were octagonal when open, and were called credence tables, implying some ecclesiastical connection). In the 1750s a 'concertina' action was used, with the frieze itself folded at each end of the table. In the 1760s the fashionable shape was rectangular with a simple moulded edge, and square-section legs replaced the elegant cabriole. The envelope table was invented in the 1780s; the top was comprised of four triangles, and by rotating the top slightly a concealed peg caused one leaf to pop up slightly, sufficiently for raising it fully, and the others likewise. The top rested on the four corners of the frieze.

A slightly unusual design was the handkerchief table (which looked like a folded handkerchief). The top consisted of two triangles which opened up to form a square. One of the legs swung out to provide support for the drop-leaf triangle. It was a simple form of gateleg that was not produced in any quantity, a variation on an old theme. But the gateleg had its limitations; as diners know to their cost, the undercarriage can get in the way of the knees, and there is a limit to the size. Why not push two occasional tables together and make a perfectly satisfactory dining table?

Thus the Georgian 'D'-end table evolved, as the name implies a semi-circular four-legged table. Pushed against an identical table it made an admirable circular or oval table, and if the table needed to be bigger there was provision for the insertion of an extra leaf. For large tables the back legs of the 'D'-end tables were moved out to help support the central section. There were a lot of ingenious methods of combining tables. Sometimes the result was all legs, but some designs had telescopic frames so that it was a simple operation to open and shut tables as required by domestic needs.

Another type of dining room table was that with more than one pedestal support. Sometimes tripods, sometimes four-legged, these are immensely popular and very expensive as they are the perfect solution to the knees-under-the-table problem. Sometimes a central leaf was inserted on a gateleg base, sometimes for long tables there were three pedestal supports. For informal dining, single pedestal tables were ideal, and for many years these were made in every conceivable style and wood, some with exquisitely inlaid work, others bulbous and carved, others elegant and splayed. Some had simple legs coming from a central turned pillar; others had a column joined to a platform from which the legs extended. There was much ingenuity displayed, and these tables also served as games tables and occasional tables right through the nineteenth century. Amongst the most-produced was the type with a triangular section set on a fairly plain frame. These are still available at reasonable prices, immensely hardy because of their no-nonsense structure.

The devotion and craftsmanship the Victorians applied to credenzas was repeated when it came to the tops of these pedestal tables, with superb marquetry, mosaic, and inlay of semi-precious stones. Spectacular woods such as yew and fine-figured walnut were much used.

There is a great variety of specialised tables. There are architects' tables which incorporate a kind of drawing-board. Some tables had fixed tops, some had tops folded back on themselves, for tea or for games; games tables often had recesses for counters or money, often with a green baize top for cards. Some tables had extensions, supported not by swinging out accessory legs but by wooden brackets fitted into the underframing. Typical of these is the Pembroke table, which has leaves on the long side, and at least one drawer with usually a dummy at the other end. In 1972, £3,900 was paid for a Pembroke table, a price that stunned the trade. The name, said Sheraton, arose from the 'lady who first gave orders for them'.

The Harlequin Pembroke had a concealed compartment fitted with drawers set in the top that worked on counterweights. Sofa tables, often used as small dining tables, had leaves at each end supported on small swinging brackets or on sliding bearers. Lyre-form detail was often used. The Sutherland table had a narrow centre section and disproportionately large leaves. All have their devotees, and fashions come and go. There was a recent demand especially by Americans for Pembroke tables, which for a time seemed to have no upper price limit, but periods of intense enthusiasm are followed by lethargy.

When buying a 'fancy' table at a realistic price it is wise to examine it very carefully, making certain that any marquetry or inlay looks right rather than like an Edwardian improvement. These tables once had very little value if they were plain, unless they were optimistically called Sheraton or Hepplewhite. Turn them upside down – not

Sheraton drawing table of 1793.

REGENCY ROSEWOOD SOFA TABLE WITH BRASS INLAY

1 If brass inlay comes out it is likely to come out in one piece, and consequently it is easier to deal with than wooden inlay. If the wood in which the brass is set shrinks or twists in any way the brass inlay is inclined to buckle up, and if it is decided that the wood be left as it is there are two ways to deal with the problem: trimming the brass to make it fit, or taking out more wood so that the brass slots in. Brass inlay can be kept in place by pins, the heads nipped off and the pins rubbed down with sandpaper so that they lie flush with the inlay. Modern adhesives need to be used when relaying brass inlay, and as brass is springy it should be cramped down while the adhesive is setting. If brass inlay is missing, it may indicate that the wood has warped some time in the past. If the inlay is part of a repeating pattern, a tracing can be made, or heel ball can be used, so that new brass sheeting can be cut to fill the gap. Brass sheeting is soft and easy to cut.

2 Brass stringing buckles up in the form of a shallow loop if there is warping in the wood. It may be sufficient to nip off a short length and relay. When taking up brass inlay do not pull, but gently prise out with a small piece of wood. If the stringing has been buckled for some time, perhaps imperceptibly, the groove may have gathered dirt and grime which needs poking out before the stringing is reinserted. Brass is often lacquered, and if it looks dingy it may help to remove the lacquer. Conversely, if replacement inlay or stringing is too bright, lacquering will tone it down.

3 The grain of the rosewood on the four feet runs horizontally and as the pressure of the full weight of the table falls on them this is the most likely part of the table to suffer a break. Because of the gentle curvature, it may be possible to use screws on the underneath side (drilling first to reduce the chance of a split), countersinking them and covering them with a small circle of rosewood veneer.

4 The castors are slotted onto the feet, and affixed with side screws. Because of the weight of the table these may work loose, and may need to be rescrewed, if necessary reinforcing the wood which may have been damaged by the movement of loose screws. In a very severe case, it is possible to shorten all the legs by an inch or so and refit the castors on fresh wood. The castors are brass on paw feet, but there is always a possibility that they may have been replaced in Victorian times by composition or china castors, which are anachronistic. It may be preferable to fit reproduction brass castors.

5 The crossbanding should be carefully checked to see if there are any segments missing. As there is no pattern in the crossbanding here, merely light and dark wood, replacement should not be difficult providing that one remembers to clean off the base wood so that the new insertion lies perfectly flush.

6 The hinges of the flaps should be checked and if the flaps are not in alignment with the top when raised, they may need to be adjusted.

7 Damage here, even if minor, will get worse if not treated immediately, and a small split, which may be cured by gluing, may turn into a break because of the dead weight of the flaps.

8 Check that all the beading is intact. It may be possible to get replacements if a few beads are missing, or new beads can be carved. An alternative is to take a pattern of one of the existing beads in plasticine or similar, and recast in plastic wood, suitably tinted to match. As there is no pressure, this method would suffice.

9 Because there are no stresses it is unlikely that the top of a sofa table of this type will split. If a sliver of veneer needs to be inserted, and a tourniquet needs to be applied lengthwise while the glue is drying, the flaps need to be removed. In this case the figuring of the table top is less dramatic than that of the flaps, and a match is easier to come by if a repair is necessary. A split in the top would greatly reduce the value of such a table, which depends to a large extent on its condition and, unlike a dining room table, is a 'fancy' piece.

Another solution to the provision of large tables, using two tripod pillars and additional leaves. This mahogany pedestal table dates from around 1800.

difficult as they are quite light – and ascertain that there are no mysterious screw holes or signs of mayhem. Examine the legs, making certain that there are no well disguised repairs. These tables can be fragile and ill-usage can affect them. If there is marquetry, ascertain that there are no pieces missing and that there are no replacement bits. If the table is 'a.f.' ('as found', auctioneers' jargon for something that needs repair), and this is reflected in a low price, work out if you can do the work yourself and if not how much it will cost to put it right. Are the leaves right for the table? Look for mouldings and grain and general finish. Solid mahogany is always easier to repair than veneer. For highly desirable pieces, such as large dining tables of whatever kind, a high degree of distress is acceptable.

The dressing table was referred to as a toilet table – the toilet was the cloth which covered the table or 'the dressing box wherein are kept the paints, pomatums, essences, patches etc; the pincushion, powder-box, brushes etc, which are esteemed parts of a lady's toilet'. So much for etymology. Many 'kneehole desks' were designed as dressing tables, but others are elegant mahogany pieces, sometimes with the most intricate superstructure and fitments. What are now used as high-quality period dressing tables were designed as sideboards (the clue lies in the cupboards at the sides).

Marble tables were popular from about 1720. At first only white marble was imported, stained to imitate more costly varieties, but about 1738 Irish and English coloured marble was quarried. Marble was always expensive, and in Italy furniture was painted to imitate marble. The most characteristic piece of marble-topped furniture in

The rococo style so prevalent in Europe had only a limited effect on English furniture – with the exception of marble-topped console tables and mirror surrounds.

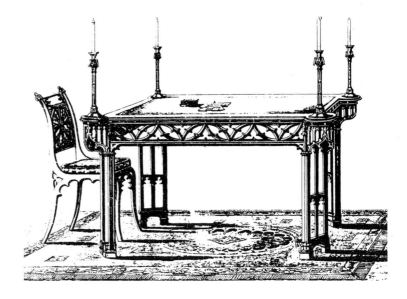

An illustration of a Gothic table in **Gothic Furniture** by A. W. N. Pugin published in 1835. Pugin saw in the Gothic style the way forward for English design.

Britain was the console table, French in feeling, and an aristocratic piece. The common-or-garden marble-topped piece of furniture was the ubiquitous Edwardian and 1920s washstand. These were bought for next to nothing in the 1960s, the marble was taken off and transferred to the iron base of a treadle sewing-machine and the washstand itself broken up for firewood. Sometimes the marble was stacked away, waiting for a nondescript piece of furniture so that a console table could be made up.

Reading tables, writing tables, and artists' tables could either be simple structures on a tripod stand or fully fledged pieces of furniture. Some of these categories are interchangeable, and all incorporate a hinged or rising board with a rest or a fillet of wood on which to set book, sketch pad, or notepaper. Some had drawers, and some were equipped with candle-holders.

Side tables can date back to the seventeenth century, and whether they were all used as side tables or multi-purpose freestanding tables is open to question. Some have been given the name 'lowboys' – often used for a dressing table – to confuse the issue and add an air of mystery to amiable, unpretentious, useful items of furniture. They all reflect the changing fashions: oak, walnut, inlay, mahogany, plus the fruitwoods, elm, and anything else that happened to be handy, and any number and arrangement of drawers is viable. In fact, 'side tables' is a catch-all category. A country-made piece with odd-looking legs. What can it be? For the kitchen? Is it for some rustic Milton? Or is it a writing table?

The writing table proper is sometimes referred to as a library table, but it is uncertain as to what its exact use was? One of the main characteristics of Georgian and Regency writing tables is that they are fitted out with substantial supports at each end rather than legs, and are masculine pieces of furniture without nonsense, though nowhere near as desirable as the round writing tables, with drawers round the perimeter. These tables are known as drum-top, though some refer to them as rent tables, as it is imaginatively supposed that accounts of rents were kept in the drawers, though no-one seems to wonder why. The supports are either in the form of a pedestal or a column on legs, sometimes three, sometimes four. Carlton House tables, named after the London home of the Prince Regent, later George IV, were illustrated in 1788, elegant rather feminine tables in satinwood or mahogany. They were often inlaid, with a range of drawers and a superstructure containing a range of fitments. Those encountered today are most likely Edwardian reproductions, which fetch high prices because they were superbly made. Some Carlton House derivatives are ungainly, with high superstructures or even a bookcase stuck on top.

Whatever ambiguities may exist in dressing tables, writing tables, and specialist tables of all kinds, there are few problems with the tripod table. It is what it is, a simple arrangement of top, column, and legs. Sometimes there is a gallery beneath the top known as a bird cage. Some tops are fixed, some fold back and line up with the column. There is sometimes a rim, in good quality tripods, in the form of a pie-crust. The column could be barrel-turned, spiral-turned, fluted, or angular. The column could rest on a platform, with much truncated feet. Tripod tables, and their close relative the four-legged or quadripod form, were not only made of wood. In the early nineteenth century papier-mâché was used and somewhat later, metal. There is a thin line separating small tripod tables from pedestal dining tables.

Tripod tables have never gone out of fashion, and country-made examples are still very reasonably priced as they were made in such huge quantities. Modern reproductions are amazingly faithful to early models, and are incredibly cheap. When their gloss has been tempered, they may cause confusion. Because they are so cheap they may be worthwhile buying for transformation purposes, their finish stripped off, and painted pastel shades.

Because of their simple structure, tripod tables have often been subject to renovation. They may be fitted out with replacement tops. With many classic tables the diameter of the top is the same as that of the area covered by the feet, but sometimes even unchanged tables can have tops that look either top-heavy or too small.

The obvious development of the tripod table is to stick something on top and turn it into something else. Thus the teapoy. 'Teapoy' means 'three [Hindi] feet [Persian]'. It is by strange coincidence that the teapoy was used for tea, brought into fashion by the wife of Charles II (Catherine of Braganza), though the first teapoys were much later. They were certainly in full production by 1820. In 1858 the teapoy was defined by Simmonds' *Dictionary of Trade* as 'an ornamental pedestal table with lifting top enclosing caddies for holding tea'. It went into disuse about this time, and was often converted to the work table. These might be better termed 'hobby tables'. Games, needlework, embroidery, all had their specialist tables on tripods, end supports with a stretcher, four legs, or platforms. Many had a bag beneath, but in the 1850s this was often replaced by a funnel. Some of the fittings are delightful, and surprisingly many of the interiors remain in marvellous condition, with the silk intact. Work tables were luxury objects with price no object, and the rare woods were frequently used, together with high-quality marquetry. As small decorative antiques, work tables seem undervalued compared with some objects of the same period that are simply not worth the money. The fakers have largely left work tables alone, as their reproduction savours of hard work.

When looking at pieces of furniture the economics of making another one should be considered. For example, the cost of the wood for a reproduction refectory table is enormous, unless some fly-by-night operator has descended to the use of old floorboards.

As with side tables, 'occasional tables' is a catch-all category. They are sometimes referred to as 'centre tables' for no very clear reason. The centre of what? A room? But why have an insignificant table in the centre of a room? Some of the most delightful of

A typical specimen of Regency 'fancy' furniture of the 1810s, a work table, or an artist's table, or indeed almost anything.

An Art Deco dressing table of about 1935 in walnut using laminated wood. The shape of the mirror is typical of the period.

Georgian tray-top commode, very useful in bedroom or drawing room.

83

these occasional tables are the Arts and Crafts specimens, obeying no laws of propriety, often in unvarnished wood, and usually containing little quirky decorative features. The most common type of late Victorian or Edwardian occasional table is the octagonal, often in mahogany, sometimes with up to eight spidery legs. The worst-selling examples are ebonised, sometimes with gilt ornament, the best are the very elegant neo-classical examples with inlay and crossbanding.

A word must be said in praise of the draw-leaf table. Scorned, banished to the tool-shed, these are occasionally dragged out and refurbished and found to be remarkably useful and well-made, with a wind-out mechanism that is all but indestructible. This can include some of the 1930s draw-leaf tables, well-made if rather ugly.

The demand for hard-wearing tables has been met by the dealers who specialise in pine. The tables they offer may not be so old as they appear, for they usually have square legs of ambiguous date and basic structure.

XV

Washstands

Victorian and Edwardian washstands remain the stock in trade of the low to middle range dealer. They are utilitarian articles of furniture, and if they are bought cheaply they might be cannibalised so that there is little trace of their former self. The tiles which were added as a splash-back around the turn of the century could be taken off and sold separately; if there was a marble top, that could be sold, even if it was black and not marble but slate; the brass towel-rail at the side was removed, worth a pound or two to someone. As for the washstand itself, the back could be neatly taken off or trimmed down, and a leather insert fitted to make a very pleasing writing table. It usually had nice turned legs, and two drawers, so was well suited to conversion.

Although the Victorian washstand bore strong similarities to those of the previous age, it was often finished off less elegantly – no cock-beading round the drawers and more boisterous turning in the legs. The Georgian corner washstand is a much more desirable article, even though it was basically a frame for holding a jug and basin. There was usually a shaped back, and a gallery section below the basin shelf could incorporate drawers. Sometimes there was a stretcher with a shaped piece to hold the jug. The basin shelf with the hole in the middle gave the game away. In no way could this elegant piece of furniture be anything but a washstand. So often this shelf is replaced, and given another one with a leather insert. It becomes a fairly useless piece of decorative furniture, but the value is enhanced. This operation is really superfluous, for the hole for the bowl makes a perfect receptacle for a crocus bowl or plant pot, and as a plant stand the corner washstand does very well indeed.

Ordinary four-legged washstands were made without much change well into the 1930s, though without the colourful Art Nouveau tiles at the back. They are very drab, and even in the 1960s there were still boarding-houses where guests at a pound or so a night were dependent for their ablutions on the jug and basin. Plumbed wash basins in the bedroom put an end to the jug and basin as well as the washstand.

European and American Furniture

XVI

European Furniture

There is more British furniture abroad than foreign furniture in Britain. Since the 1960s great quantities of furniture have been exported from the UK, and this includes high-quality French furniture which the aristocracy imported into the UK in the eighteenth and nineteenth centuries. There is foreign furniture in the UK which has no English equivalent, such as the Spanish cabinets with a multitude of tiny drawers, and as continental furniture design in the seventeenth century was well ahead of British, unusual items of furniture can be considerably older than at first appears.

At a time when British furniture was in the transitional state from oak to walnut, and foreign influences were beginning to be apparent, French furniture was well proportioned, clearly designed, and refined. When Louis XIV came to the throne in 1661 these qualities were retained, with added opulence. Many of the terms used in French furniture such as commode, armoire, bureau, fauteuil, chaise, were Anglicised.

In the eighteenth century there was a move away from the formality of Versailles to the ease and free-living of Paris, and furniture became lighter and more frivolous, without being less well made. Until 1791 Paris furniture-making was presided over by stern guilds dating from the Middle Ages. From 1743 makers were obliged to stamp their names on their work, and it was also stamped with the letters JME to show that it had passed the scrutiny of the guild. By 1720 veneers were in kingwood, purplewood, and tulipwood, and the French developed their own form of lacquer, called *vernis Martin*. A favourite shape for the French commode (a form of chest of drawers) was *bombé* (swollen) and this was a challenge to those who applied marquetry.

A curious diversion from good taste and proportions was the rococo craze, reaching a pitch in the 1730s, in which violent asymmetry was the rule rather than the exception. This had an effect on English mirrors, but not on much else in English furniture; rococo was nevertheless a widespread phenomenon throughout much of Europe, though countries such as Holland resisted it as frivolous. French social life was regulated by women, and furniture reflects their preferences. So there were innumerable types of chairs suited for every kind of formal or informal situation, as well as sofas (and beds).

In Italy the speciality was carved gilded softwood, ideal for rococo, but regional styles were far more important than in France and England. Roman furniture was rich but sober, Venetian furniture was exuberant, and Neapolitan furniture was top-heavy and bizarre. German regional styles were also varied, open to outside influences and the settlement of French furniture-makers. Much depended on the personal preferences of the multitude of princes and monarchs.

VICTORIAN WALNUT EBONISED CENTRE TABLE (LOUIS XV STYLE)

1 The legs, being slender and in cabriole form, are especially vulnerable, and a break may be camouflaged by the gilt-metal mounts, which could very well act as a kind of splint. A bad break would be difficult to repair as it would mean taking off the mounts. Without close examination of the actual piece of furniture the quality of the mounts is difficult to gauge, though because of the obvious quality of the piece it is likely to be good. The most vulnerable part of the leg is the ankle, which, due to the direction of the grain, always has a tendency to snap. The legs are ebonised, which in 1870 was a fashionable finish, but ebonising can conceal any defects in the underlying wood.

2 There is high-quality inlay in the frieze and on the top, and this should be examined very closely, as it is easier to fill in naturalistic marquetry rather than geometric parquetry. So the floral motifs on the frieze should make botanical sense. A missing piece may have been replaced by a piece which 'would do' and would not be intrusive. It is worthwhile seeing if the inlaid pieces are hand-cut rather than mechanically cut (machine-cut pieces are more symmetrical), though this would not add or detract from the value.

3 Check that the aprons have not been tampered with and are the same all the way round. If a section is damaged it is always possible that it has been trimmed, and the rest of the apron made to match. Ebonising would help hide this.

4 Check that the drawer runs well, and take it out to see if there is any damage to the linings (the sides). If there is wobble it may mean that the runners need attention – a simple job; if it goes back too far it may mean that the stops are missing, easily added. The small dimensions of the table mean that the interior may not give a woodworker much room to manoeuvre.

5 If there is damage to the gilt-metal mounts, it might be more convenient to do a cosmetic repair as the mounts serve a decorative and not a functional purpose. It may be possible to find out what metal has been gilded, whether bronze or an inferior metal. If the damage is superficial – perhaps discolouration – Goldfinger, bought in the tube and rubbed on with the finger-tip or a soft cloth, may be sufficient.

6 The top of this table is also inlaid, and is more likely to show damage than the friezes. A split may be an indication of wear or of warping, but because of the structure any warping would not be significant, and a split may be repaired by filling with wax or the insertion of a sliver of veneer. As with the frieze, naturalistic inlay is more easily repaired than geometric.

7 Ebonising is often more brown than black, and if an area is rubbed it is possible to use shoe-polish to blend with the surrounding sections.

In France, rococo was relatively short-lived, and there was a return to good proportions, rather too much so, with a preoccupation with what was thought the Greek style where the furniture was ponderous and severe. In the 1770s furniture was gentler, with linear shapes, and much use of lacquer and marquetry, with ormolu mounts protecting the corners of furniture. In the 1780s the French became interested in English furniture, with the widespread use of mahogany veneer, but used with plaques and ormolu so that the appearance was very un-English. Then came the Revolution and the period known as Directoire (about 1790–1800), in which economy was combined with traditional flair: less veneer, ormolu, and marquetry, and furniture became less weighty (as in England). The Directoire period was followed by the

Detail of an Art Nouveau washstand, with characteristic tiled splash-back.

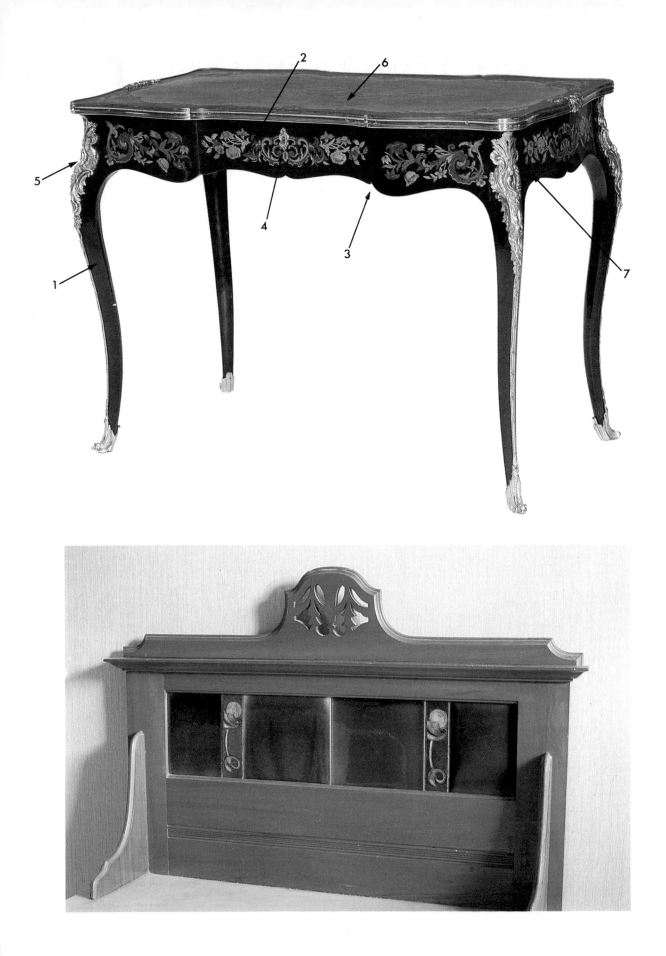

Consulat and Empire periods: Napoleonic furniture, monumental, portentous, for display and not comfort. Ormolu returned, no longer to protect vulnerable parts, but as a blatant decoration demanding attention. Egyptian motifs were popular, as they were in England. After about 1815 contours were softened. Furniture became more homely. The grand gesture was out of favour.

As communications between countries became easier, even during wars, styles and influences were exchanged; shield-back chairs, for example, of English parentage, appear in Italy as well as Scandinavia. Certain countries clung to their heritage, such as Spain and Austria, irrespective of their occupation by foreigners. In Germany what is known as the Biedermeier style became important, and is today much sought after, despite unkind things that have been said about it. John Gloag wrote in his *Short Dictionary of Furniture* (1952):

> A style of furnishing and interior decoration, exuberantly vulgar, that originated in Germany during the second decade of the nineteenth century and became popular among the new and tasteless rich classes of England and Europe. Opulently carved furniture loaded with embossed metal ornament, caricatured the French Empire style, and black horsehair, frequently used for upholstery, contrasted vividly with gilt mounts.

Twenty years later the respected writer on furniture, Edward Joy in his *Connoisseur Guide to Furniture* described it as 'quiet and well-mannered'. A drastic reassessment. To purists, the Biedermeier style ends in 1830, but to others it covers the period 1814–49.

Mahogany and oak were out of fashion, and in came walnut, light birch, ash, fruitwoods (pear and cherry). The grain was visible, and maple and other similar

Each time fashionable styles were reproduced, tiny differences reflected the spirit of the age. This 'Louis XVI' fauteuil chair is neither French nor Louis XVI (1754–93) but was made about 1880. It is as finely crafted as an original.

The craze for Chinese decorative details resulted in Chippendale fretwork and imitation bamboo, as in this Regency chair.

A rather sober walnut side table of about 1730 which is in fact Dutch and has a stolid quality lacking in English furniture of the period.

A very busy marquetry cabinet with gilt fittings, certainly continental.

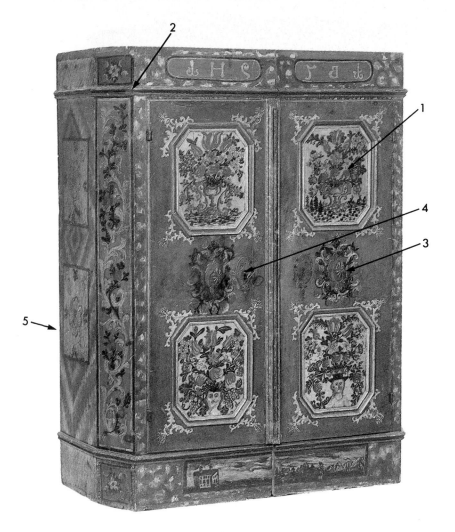

TYROLEAN PAINTED ARMOIRE

1 Continental furniture such as this armoire dating from 1791 may present a challenge to those accustomed only to English or French furniture. In particular the extent of the painting may bemuse.

2 The construction of such pieces is usually basic, and jointing is often crude. Sometimes the makers rely on the weight of the structure to hold things together, and armoires with a cornice can provide a nasty experience. If the cornice is removed the whole thing can fall apart.

3 The quality of the painting is often naive, and many pine dealers think that they can price up their ambiguous wardrobes and similar pieces by painting pictures on them, which they then age by sandpapering down. They often fall down on this because some believe that naive means simple-minded and incompetent.

4 The locks and the hinges are often a clue to the genuineness of a piece of this nature. The hinges are usually strap-hinges, and if suitably distressed they can look considerably older than they are. The locks are usually ornate.

5 An all-over painting finish, as in this example, can cover woodworm damage and it is more realistic to examine the wood on the inside or on the back. The interior may be part-shelved or completely empty, except for a bar on which to hang clothes.

woods were used for inlay. The style was characterised by simple straight lines, and the joints of rails and legs were openly displayed. The aim was comfort with dignity; sizes were scaled down, and taller pieces were not above eye-level. After 1830 the backs, arms and legs of furniture appeared to be modelled from some soft material.

In both England and France from the 1830s onwards there was a Romantic revival, first of all Gothic, and then earlier native styles. This could result in the copy of a copy, as in the English Louis Philippe style. In Russia a reworking of classic French chairs and tables of the 1730 period produced magnificent specimens using malachite as a veneer. A suite of these was sent to Chatsworth in 1844. With the popularity of international exhibitions from 1851 onwards, national styles converged towards a general European style, with woodworking machinery and short-cuts increasingly used. European furniture tended to exude an air of comfort.

Of course there were intermittent reactions against this. The Arts and Crafts and Aesthetic movements, which included a craze for all things oriental and involved a revival of bamboo and lacquer, had their counterparts in Europe, and Art Nouveau had many manifestations. French Art Nouveau furniture had no parallel in Britain. Knobbly, congested, looking more like plant forms or the skeletons of prehistoric monsters than furniture, it was enormously expensive.

After World War I, the lead in innovatory modern furniture was taken by the Germans and the Scandinavians. Britain was struggling out of post-Edwardian *ennui* and its furniture was cosy and chintzy, French furniture was extravagant and exotic, and bleak functional furniture from Europe laid claim to be the furniture of the future. Le Corbusier and his crew were defining houses as machines for living in.

The ultimate ideal was the one-piece object made in one process. A plywood table of 1935 was the first fruit; in the late 1940s a child's chair of moulded plywood was made all in one piece; the first one-piece table in plastic was designed in Germany in 1959; the Germans made a one-piece plastic armchair in 1963 and it seemed that plastics would conquer all. But not the furniture retailers in the high street, nor their customers. And probably not the ordinary man in the street in Paris, Milan, or Dusseldorf. Traditions linger longer with the consumer than the designer.

XVII

American Furniture

In the early days America was a land of regions and different nationalities who brought their own languages and traditions with them – and their ideas of what constituted good furniture. The Dutch colonised the Hudson valley, the Germans settled in Pennsylvania, and the English moved into the far south and New England. Little American furniture survives from the seventeenth century, unlike Britain, where seventeenth-century furniture is still a staple of the London auction rooms. Early American furniture was rugged, functional and without frills except for some decorative turning, but by the late seventeenth century American furniture-makers were copying European, mostly English, furniture. What is known as the American Colonial style was marked by simplicity, combination-furniture (such as the table

This cabinet of the 1860s is typical of the heavy prestige pieces that were once thought the essence of Victoriana. The obsession with decoration for the sake of decoration is often thought of as peculiarly English, but nineteenth-century American furniture could be even more laden with extraneous detail.

93

A French Empire escritoire of about 1810, though it could be called almost anything. A very plain exterior, compensated for by extravagant figuring in the mahogany. There is a fall front revealing the usual drawers and an arched recess. Below are two doors concealing three long drawers. Despite its period and its basic usefulness its lack of charm brings its value down to around £2,000.

An Art Deco smoker's table of the 1930s, once of no regard, but now collected, if they are well-made and are somehow distinctive and can be pressed into modern use.

which served as a chair and vice versa) and the use of native woods, such as maple, hickory and, of course, pine. Pine was not a lowly wood to frontiersmen.

With sophistication and the rise of an urban élite, furniture became more elegant, and paralleled that of Europe, except that there was less opulence and formality. As in Britain, the introduction of mahogany brought in furniture particularly suited to the wood – elegant, strong, easily carved. When Neoclassicism swept through Europe, America was not immune, but the orthodox motifs, the husks, the swags, the urns were supplemented to include the eagle. This period produced perhaps the best-known American cabinet-maker of all time, Duncan Phyfe, as famous in the USA as Chippendale.

One interesting characteristic of American furniture is that many communities kept themselves to themselves, and persisted in using and making furniture which belonged to a previous age. The Shakers continued to use eighteenth-century models long after everyone else had discarded them, modifying them and improving them. And immigrants with their own furniture heritage continued to prefer and use that which was to their taste, whether or not it was out of fashion. But mostly, styles in Europe

Although described as a commode, this is a straightforward chest-of-drawers of about 1770, given additional charm and value by being serpentine fronted. The chunky bracket feet are later additions. This may be American, where English furniture styles were followed quite faithfully.

An Art Deco ensemble, especially popular in America where the 'cinema foyer' style of furnishing flourished.

were mirrored in America. American Gothic was even less like the real thing than in Europe, because most Americans did not know what genuine Gothic was. The American version of Victorianism could be even more tortuous than it was in the UK. And they could produce it more cheaply and on a massive scale because of their pre-eminence in mass-production techniques.

Perhaps the most recognisable of American pieces of furniture is what is known as the Wells Fargo desk, more properly the Wootton Patent Office desk or Wootton for short. This was a desk which opened up from the front, revealing a multitude of drawers and pigeon holes on the opening side (or sides, for sometimes there was a double door) as well as in the orthodox fall-front desk itself. It was usually made in American walnut, often with heavy carving on the superstructure, and panelled doors. The first were made about 1870, and they have an aura of method and efficiency, though no doubt they were ideal to lose things in.

Surprisingly, America, despite the adventurous furniture made by Frank Lloyd Wright in the 1890s and 1900s, was not a market leader in modern furniture and like Britain, was the influenced rather than the influencer. The furniture was glossy and streamlined, as evident from studio sets in films from the 1930s, but the self-conscious modernism often concealed tired ideas. It was show furniture, suitable for cinema foyer or hotel vestibule. But in 1940 the Museum of Modern Art in New York ran a competition for 'Organic Design in Home Furnishings'. First prize was won by an all-one-piece chair, and this created great interest in moulded plywood and, later, moulded plastic and fibreglass, leading to the influential 'womb chair'. A chair was no longer a seat, a back, and legs; a table was no longer a piece of flat wood with legs. Furniture was being seen anew.

American furniture often incorporated the eagle as a decorative feature. However, this is a green-marbled-top console table made in England in the William Kent tradition.

PART II

THE PRACTICAL
ASPECTS

Repairing and Restoring Your Furniture

Repairing and refurbishing furniture requires commonsense more than anything else. It is important for the reader to realise his or her limitations and not to take on work that calls for twenty years of experience, but, having said this, most basic jobs can be carried out using a narrow range of tools, most of which can be found in the average garage or workshed. It is important to think the job through from beginning to end; never take off with vast enthusiasm without visualising the later stages. It is all very well taking out a piece of damaged veneer, but is the replacement piece exactly right? Does the grain run the right way? Or is it new veneer which is much thinner than the old wood, and should really be at least two slices thick?

Think about what might happen if the job goes wrong. Can the work you have done on the piece of furniture be reversed? If you have filled in a split in a table-top and are not happy with it, can you take out the filling and try again? If you have used the traditional methods, you can. Waxes and other fillings merely need to be heated, probably only with the quick application of a domestic iron over a towel. If the split was a wide one you may have inserted a fillet of veneer sideways, and filled up around it. Again, the filling can be softened and removed, and the fillet can be delicately prised out without causing any damage.

However, if you have been experimenting with modern materials there may be problems. The filling material may have set like granite and need gouging out, causing damage to the surrounding wood. If instant glue has been used (instead of Scotch glue or PVA), a straightforward job can turn into a nightmare. One should always think carefully before using such quick-acting adhesives, though it is always tempting – especially when the wood to be worked on needs clamping down or the application of weights while the ordinary glue sets.

With some structural repairs you may have a second chance. If you are repairing an upholstered chair, fixing it up with brackets which will be hidden from sight, you can abort the process at any time and start again. But if you are taking out a section of a chair rail and fixing in a new piece, as soon as the saw bites into the wood you are committed and there is no going back. It is always vital to look ahead and anticipate your next move.

There is an old saying 'If it works, don't fix it.' If the piece of furniture you are working on is antique or reasonably old a certain degree of distress is acceptable. A broken lock in a Victorian chest-of-drawers may be a nuisance, but is it vital to put it right? However, a lock on a desk which doesn't work is another matter; the desk may *need* to be locked. Another typical everyday problem is an ink-stain on the leathered top of a valuable desk such as a Davenport. One can no longer buy a Davenport for as little as forty pounds as one could twenty years ago – you would have to pay at least a thousand pounds, and an ink stain now detracts only marginally from its value. So what do you do? Do you treat it with household bleach or the other methods outlined in the following sections or do you re-leather the top? The latter may sound like a safer option, but how will the new leather look in its context? Will it outshine the faded walnut? Will you have to face the prospect of distressing the new leather top so that it fits in?

Every repair job needs more than a little thought and always more time than you think at first you will need. If it is a fairly major structural task and you have limited experience of woodwork, it is not a bad idea to practise on a piece of fairly worthless furniture. You may have a nice chair which has got woodworm in a leg, a section of which needs to be taken out and replaced. A basic 1930s dining-room chair can be bought very cheaply, and this can be used to experiment on.

Cleaning and polishing wood is almost wholly without problems, though you may have to consider whether certain pieces of furniture should or should not be French polished. Opinions vary on what might be called 'the state of shine': eighteenth-century furniture may look very striking when made as bright as a button, but many prefer the quiet mellow look, bearing in mind that French polishing had never even been heard of during the eighteenth century. Basic treatment of furniture is very simple: a clean surface can be achieved with a vinegar and water mix, and added protection is easily given if wood is waxed, followed by a good dosing of elbow grease. Many restorers of the old school adhere to this regimen and reject more up-to-date ideas on the treatment of wood, but as you own the furniture it is entirely up to you how you like to see it presented.

Furniture does not, however, consist entirely of wood: there are often brass and other metal fittings, especially in Regency and Victorian showpieces such as credenzas and chiffoniers. If a section of a brass-fretted gallery on a desk or cabinet is missing it cries out to be repaired; if a finial is missing it is ridiculous to leave it so. But minor defects, such as a battered brass knob or a dent in a brass column, may often be left as they are without detracting from the look of the piece. Indeed, many a time more harm than good has been done to a piece in trying to repair such small blemishes, and some people actually *like* to see signs of age and wear, as, when so much furniture of the past is being reproduced, these are indications of authenticity – and value.

The tools and equipment really needed in repairs and refurbishment are few, but if you are going to do a considerable number of repairs make certain they are of good quality. Cutting edges, whether they be those of saws, chisels, or planes, should be as sharp as possible. For routine work use the variety of electrical tools and gadgets now on the market and increasing in scope every year – there is no innate virtue in using hand-tools for the sake of using them. You can, of course, build up a collection of exotic one-purpose tools, such as moulding planes, and these can be found, with little difficulty, second-hand at boot sales, fairs, street markets and flea markets at very low prices.

Repairing and restoring furniture can be as adventurous as you like. And if you like adventure you may like to try 'transforming' furniture, turning an ordinary worthless object into something new and exotic – making wood look like marble or malachite, or maybe even making marble and malachite look like wood! Here, all the products of modern technology are open to you, and for once it does not matter if the processes cannot be reversed. Transformation furniture is fun and this, of course, is the most important prerequisite of good furniture repair and restoration – it should be fun! Enjoy yourselves!

XVIII

Tools

The tools needed for repairs to furniture are quite few in number, and this is a basic list which can be added to at will. There are certain useful tools which can be made, such as a screwdriver with a sharpened end, ideal for such jobs as scraping out the remnants of old dowels and tenons. The operator may prefer to work on a firm table, or use the excellent Workmate. The range of powered tools is now very wide, and includes drills, circular saws, jigsaws, and, very useful, the orbital sander.

Bench vice The antique restorer's most basic and indispensable tool.

Bits These can be round ended or square ended (which fit only into the hand-operated brace). They include: the twist bit, standard for metalwork but also used for woodwork; the auger bit, which has a projecting centre spur to allow drill point to be centred; the countersink bit, a conical bit available in angles of 90°, 65°, 60°, and 45° to cut depressions so that screws can be sunk; the centre bit, which cuts shallow holes; the screwdriver bit, which inserted into a drill acts as a powerful screwdriver; the Jennings bit, which is a double spiral cutter; and the single spiral bit, which makes for rapid work though perhaps it is less accurate than the Jennings.

Bradawl For starting screws off. There is also the gimlet. It is often more convenient to use any odd instrument handy, such as the pointed blade of a pair of scissors, but this does not make for accuracy, as even the tiniest error may throw the work out.

Chisels Bevel edged, for general paring work. Firmer chisels, with rectangular cross-section, for heavier work. Mortice chisels, for use with a mallet. Most woodworkers prefer wooden-handled chisels, but plastic handles are useful when a mallet is being used.

Cork sanding block This is optional. Some workers in wood prefer to use their glass-paper in a pad or wrapped round a wooden block.

Cramps The G-cramp is the standard cramp (clamp in America), which is self-descriptive. Some have a 'wide throat' for holding more substantial work. The sash cramp comprises two adjustable shoes on a long bar. One slides along the bar, and is fixed with a pin; the other is a miniature vice. The bar can be home-made. Sash cramps come in various sizes.

Files Flat, round, half round, which come in all sizes. It is easy to use a certain file through habit without realising that it has worn down and is not doing its job. The rat-tail file can be very useful for fiddling jobs that seem to cry out for a specialist tool.

Gouges Made in various sizes and useful if any carving needs to be done. Very handy for clearing out grime and old varnish from mouldings.

Hammers The traditional hammer with a claw can be very useful, but a soft-headed (rubber or nylon) hammer is desirable where wood is involved as it will not leave marks. Where a metal hammer-head is used, a piece of wood should be inserted between the head and the hammered surface. The upholsterer's hammer is a lightweight hammer for driving in tacks and gimp pins.

Mallet Essential for use with wooden-handled tools.

Marking gauge Marks out parallel lines, using a projecting pin. This pin can be replaced with a sharp cutting instrument, and used for taking out old stringing.

Nail punch To drive nails or pins below surface. Very useful, but it must be remembered that a nail or pin sunk below the wood surface is extremely difficult to remove.

Oilslip A shaped stone for sharpening gouges and the irons of moulding planes.

Oilstone A visit to an ironmonger to have tools sharpened can be an expensive business, and chisels in particular have to be kept sharp.

Pincers Mainly used for removing nails from surfaces.

Planes Metal planes are often advised, but many amateurs prefer the old-fashioned wooden planes. A smoothing plane is essential, and a rebate plane to cut rebates in the edges of timber (so that glass or panels can be inserted) and a grooving plane are useful, along with moulding planes. These can be picked up for very small amounts of money at general markets and boot sales, and even if they are not used very often they are worth getting, considering how cheap they are.

Pliers Small pincers for bending or cutting metal.

Rasps Circular, and semi-circular, made for two-handed use.

Saws The most useful general-purpose saw is probably the tenon saw, which has a brass or steel plate across the top to give rigidity. For cutting larger pieces of timber the ordinary handsaw is better, but consideration should be given to power-operated circular saws for tiresome mundane work. These give a distinctive finish, unlike that of a hand saw. Back saws are small saws for fine work, and the dovetail saw is a smaller version of the tenon saw. The hacksaw is a useful multi-purpose tool. There are a variety of saws for cutting curves and intricate shapes, involving a thin blade held vertically under tension, such as the fretsaw, and the bow saw. The keyhole saw is also known as a padsaw, and is a narrow toothed blade set into a handle, useful to get at places other saws can't, but laborious in use.

Screwdrivers A range should be kept, including small ones such as electrical screwdrivers for use on metalwork such as small locks, and of course a ratchet screwdriver can save a lot of time.

Detail on an eighteenth-century chest of a kind that could only be produced with basic tools such as chisels and gouges.

Sliding bevel Similar to a try-square, but with this it is possible to mark out different angles on wood.

Spokeshave A two-handed instrument with a small blade which acts as a precision plane and is used with the grain.

Surform A plane with a rasp-like surface, used for coarse work before final finishing with plane, spokeshave, and glasspaper.

Swing brace Despite the electric drill, still very useful. The best are those with a ratchet mechanism.

Try-square A simple tool comprising a metal blade set at right angles to a handle, useful for marking out right angles.

Wheelbrace The ordinary hand-drill, operated by turning a handle on the side. It cannot be used with the force of a swing brace, but many people find that it can be used with more precision.

XIX

Materials

Some materials used in woodworking, repair, and general rehabilitation are of great antiquity, and have not been bettered. They are constantly being added to. Some of the new products are invaluable, but others, such as instant glue, have their drawbacks, as repairs carried out using them cannot always be reversed. However, there are products which have turned out to be not so formidable as first supposed, and traditional antidotes such as methylated spirits again come in useful on contemporary wonder products. Very rarely is there one 'best' method. For every process advocated with enthusiasm by a professional, there are at least two or three others, with their own train of supporters. Some restorers use glasspaper for a specific task; others use steel wool (erroneously called 'wire wool' by some). Despite this, a summary of commonly-used materials is a useful aid to the enthusiast.

Abrasives Used to tidy up wood. The best-known is glasspaper, which comes in various grades, the finest being flour paper. It can be used in a pad, or around a cork or wooden block. Garnet paper is sand-coated, not so easy to obtain from the local ironmonger as glasspaper, but more flexible. Wet and dry paper is the popular name of resin-bonded carbide paper. Used dry, it performs the same role as glasspaper; used damp, but not saturated, it is useful for rubbing down wood between coats of whatever is being applied. Crocus powder is a fine abrasive, and so is jewellers' rouge. Steel wool, used recklessly, can cause more damage than the other abrasives, and preference should be given to the finer grades.

Acetic acid The basis of vinegar, and the terms are used synonymously. Useful for stain removing. Distilled or white vinegar should be used, not malt, cider, wine, or three hundred other varieties.

Woodworking tools have altered little over the centuries, and a modern worker in wood can appreciate the skills exhibited in the acanthus-leaf knees of the legs of this George I chair and the precision of the ball-and-claw feet.

Acetone A strong stripper derived from petrol. Its odour is dangerous, and it is also highly flammable. It should only be used as a last resort for stubborn paint, but its action can be halted by paraffin, and slowed down by the addition of white spirit.

Adhesives The traditional woodworking adhesive is Scotch glue, applied hot. Casein glue comes in powder and is mixed in water, good for woodwork, but hardens below 20°C (58°F). It may stain some woods and if it penetrates through the veneer it is likely to cause discoloration. Cellulose adhesives are general purpose quick-drying adhesives, mostly coming in tubes. Contact adhesives are strong, but as the name implies joined surfaces cannot be adjusted once the substance has been applied, and mistakes cannot easily be rectified. Epoxy resins come in a two-part pack, a resin and a hardener, and the best-known is Araldite, strong and versatile, widely used in china repairs, and sometimes used as a filler in wood, suitably tinted. Polyvinyl acetate emulsion (PVA) is white, colourless when dry, useful and clean in not too strenuous gluing jobs. Urea formaldehyde adhesives resist moisture and are immediate acting. For relaying leather on writing tables and desks paperhangers' paste is used, at twice the recommended solution.

Alcohol A solvent for paints and varnishes. Pure alcohol is less popular than its diluted form, methylated spirit, at least for woodworking purposes.

Alkanet root Beaten into fragments with a hammer and used in the eighteenth century with linseed oil to treat mahogany, giving it the popular reddish tinge.

Ammonia Useful for removing grease and dirt, varnish and paint, and is used for darkening wood, either with a brush or by utilising its pungent fumes. Fumed oak was much used by the Victorians.

Aniline dyes These can be dissolved in turpentine or water depending on the type bought, and are used for staining wood, both solid and veneers. The best-known is Vandyke brown, often called just Vandyke. Almost any colour wood can be obtained by mixing dyes.

Asphaltum Dissolved in turpentine makes a satisfactory darkening agent for wood.

Beaumontage A filler composed of beeswax rosin and shellac.

Beeswax The traditional furniture wax, used in conjunction with other substances not only for waxing but for filling holes in wood and general refurbishment.

Bichromate of potash A useful staining medium.

Bleach Domestic bleach is used for stain-removing, and more formidable concoctions for lightening the colour of woods. A mild bleach is oxalic acid dissolved in water.

Brick dust Used in the eighteenth century with linseed oil as a colouring agent for mahogany. Now oddly neglected.

Butter of antimony A minor ingredient in one recipe for a reviver.

Camphorated oil Often used as a substitute for linseed oil.

Candlegrease Used for easing moving parts of furniture such as drawers.

Carbon tetrachloride Some wood such as rosewood has a slightly greasy nature, and may be resistant to gluing. Carbon tetrachloride is a de-greasing agent, not to be used lightly as it is poisonous.

Carnauba wax A wax from Brazil, often added to beeswax to make it harder.

Caustic soda Used for stripping furniture, particularly pine.

Crocus powder A fine abrasive powder which can be lightly dusted over polished surfaces to tone them down.

French polish Shellac dissolved in methylated spirits.

Graphite Also known as plumbago and black lead, and used as a lubricant for locks and other metalwork.

Household soda Dissolved in water, darkens oak and mahogany.

Linseed oil Made from the crushed seed of flax, linseed oil is an element in oil varnishes, and is used as finish, applied in many coats at regular intervals.

Methylated spirit Invaluable for woodworkers, it is composed of ethyl alcohol, methyl alcohol, fusel oil, paraffin oil, and dye, and is used as a multi-purpose solvent.

Nitric acid Can be used to remove ink-stains.

Oil varnishes Resins dissolved in linseed oil and turpentine.

Oxalic acid An acid sold in crystal form, used for removing stains.

Paraffin Also known as kerosene, it is a grease solvent and in wax form is often used as a constituent in wax polishes.

Permanganate of potash A colouring agent, but erratic, and the wood may inexplicably change colour.

Plaster of paris A fine gypsum powder, used (tinted) as a a grain filler, but not robust enough to be used as a general purpose wood filler.

Plastic wood Used as a filler, and can be used to reconstruct broken carvings and mouldings. When hard it can be treated as wood, but it will never fool the expert.

Polyurethane lacquer Water, heat, and spirit resistant, and thus has an edge on the traditional finishes in those respects, but only those. Easily applied to anything that stands still, giving a shiny gloss that makes even the most extrovert French polishing look restrained. Very good for modern coffee tables.

Pumice powder Used as a mild adhesive.

Revivers A term used for smartening up a furniture finish. The simplest is vinegar and water; 'half-and-half' is linseed oil and white spirit with a dash of vinegar.

Rosin The solid result of distilling oil of turpentine from crude turpentine, and a constituent of Beaumontage filling.

Spirit varnish The best-known, and almost the only one known, is French polish. A gum or resin dissolved in methylated spirits.

Stains Stains come in a multitude of forms, one of the best-known being Vandyke crystals, soluble in water.

Stick stopping Used for filling holes, looks like sealing-wax, and acts like sealing-wax. It is dripped into the hole under heat (using a soldering iron/heated screwdriver).

Turpentine A solvent and a valuable constituent of waxes obtained from the juices of the pine tree.

Vinegar Used as acetic acid.

White spirit Also known as turpentine substitute, and used in exactly the same way. It is cheaper than turpentine.

XX

Structural Repairs

Repair as soon as possible. That is the cardinal rule, for if there is a fault in the piece of furniture it will throw strain on other parts of the article, especially if it is something like a chair. If a breakage is new the edges of the break will be sharper and cleaner, and easier to join. Any pieces which chip off should immediately be put on one side, preferably in a tin or, if small, an envelope, and labelled.

Chairs are very vulnerable to breakage and general wear. How often have we seen people balancing on the back legs of a chair? This applies immense pressure on the joints, and the result is inevitably that the back of the chair becomes loose, and if left there is a good chance of a breakage of some kind. If it is a chair with slats or rungs in the back these may very well work loose. Often, the offending part can be reglued into place without the necessity of dismantling the chair, though as the structure of a chair is so simple there are few problems in taking one to pieces, if it is not upholstered.

When gluing slats and rungs glue one end firmly, but not the other. Freedom and flexibility result in less strain. If a rung is too loose, insert a fine wedge, perhaps a piece of veneer, before gluing. If it is broken, it may be possible to mend it by gluing, or failing that many rungs are simple enough to make with a minimum of expertise. Buy a dowel from an ironmonger, and shape with a surform plane or smoothing plane, finishing off with a spokeshave. Most rungs have a slight taper, and a new one can be modelled on one of the existing ones. There are suppliers who provide all kinds of turned members at a reasonable cost, but those who intend to do a lot of repair and renovation should seriously consider purchasing a lathe.

When a chair needs to be dismantled, and the various components need to be knocked apart, never strike the wood directly with a mallet or hammer, but interpose a batten of flat wood. This spreads the force of the blow. A mallet is always preferable to a hammer when used with wood, and if a hammer is used it should be a rubber-headed one, or a cloth should be wrapped round the hammer head.

A surprising number of chairs have had their legs cut down, often because the feet have become damaged or have rotted away. This greatly reduces their value, and if the legs of a chair seem too short it may be that this is the reason. It is often easier to put new legs in to replace those which are badly damaged, than to mend the originals,

Sometimes it is tempting to brighten furniture up, but this would be a tragedy for this George I walnut lowboy, which could be degraded by unsympathetic French polishing.

especially if they belong to workaday chairs of no great value. Glue may be sufficient to repair a leg that is broken, but a glued leg is naturally weak and it might be better to drill a hole, and insert a dowel, especially if it is a clean break and the damaged ends slot into each other nicely. When drilling through the two parts of a broken leg it is important that the hole is centred, and it is a good idea to do a test boring with a small calibre bit using a long nail with its head sawn off to make certain that the direction of the dowel is right, and that it will slot into the drill holes when they are made. Also many chairs have legs which to some degree splay out, and this has to be taken into account during the course of any repairs.

Dowels are, of course, glued in, and should be sawn along their length to provide a channel so that surplus glue and air can escape. The length of the new dowel can be tested by inserting a pencil in the hole. It is better to cut a new dowel too long than too short, for a piece can always be taken off whereas if a dowel is too short there is an inherent weakness.

A breakage near the foot of a chair leg can perhaps be repaired by inserting a long screw, preferably one that is countersunk, so that all traces of the repair can be hidden beneath a plug, perhaps made from a flat cylinder of dowelling or from wax. Castors on chair legs should always be checked, for if they are loose there is great pressure on the wood, often causing it to split in several places. Castors can slot onto a leg, fixed by small screws, or they have a long screw. If they need to be replaced, it is important that they are in keeping. The wheels of castors can be made of various materials – brass, brown composition, or porcelain being the most common, and if just one castor needs replacing it is better to replace all four rather than put in one which is 'nearly right'.

Repairing a chair or table leg.

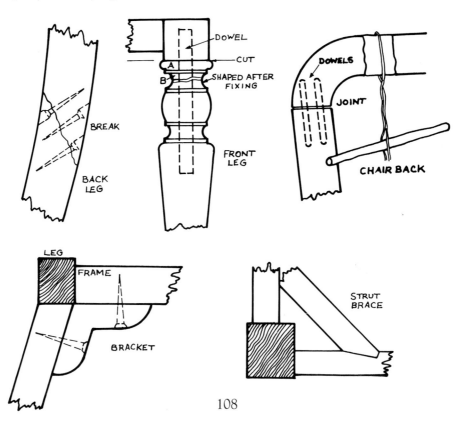

When the base of the leg is split in several places, and the castor has been taken off or has fallen off, look for signs of previous repair such as screw holes and vestiges of ancient glue. If the split is extensive, and it is clear that gluing will not work any more, the end of the chair leg needs to be neatly sawn off to the good wood, and a new part dowelled to the end, with a 'spigot' at the end to match the replaced part. Turned legs are far easier to deal with than those which have a square section, are tapered, or are cabriole.

While repairs are being carried out, even if it is merely gluing to keep the chair in operation, the broken end can be kept rigidly in place by the use of the invaluable jubilee clip, a metal band-clip tightened by a screw. The damage caused by a screw-type castor may be merely the enlargement of the hole, in which case it may be sufficient to drill out the feathery wood and insert a dowel, which, when thoroughly glued, will provide a safe housing for the castor screw. Sometimes reinforcement can be provided by a metal band, which can be painted so that it blends in with the colour of the wood, but this detracts from the value of good-quality furniture.

It is sometimes necessary to remove a dowel from a piece of furniture. Chisel off the head of the dowel, and then, using a small bit, drill a hole, as a starter. Then drill a larger hole. If uncertain how far to go, hold the drill outside the member you are dealing with, using it as an extempore rule, and work out how far the dowel extends. Wrap a piece of sticky tape around the upper part of the drill bit, near the chuck, to act as a guide. When you have drilled down to where you think the dowel ends – and it doesn't matter if it is not quite exact, for the main object is not to drill right the way through so that the bit protrudes through the outside of the wood you are drilling – stop. Cut away the debris of the rest of the dowel with some convenient tool. This could be a sharpened screwdriver. Dowels are also very useful for plugging screw holes which have become too large. They need not be too tight a fit – and when a dowel too large is hammered into its socket there is always a danger of splitting the surrounding wood – because a new screw put in the dowel will naturally expand to fill the hole.

The professional way to repair a chair leg which is badly damaged is to cut out the damaged section and insert replacement wood. This often means dismantling the chair to start with, and placing the leg in a vice. It also means a drastic reduction in the value of the chair, no matter how cleverly the colour and graining of the wood is matched. If a piece of wood is spliced in, a dovetail should be cut into it to give strength, and the new piece should be made before the old damaged section is taken out, so that a visual comparison can be made. Legs of square section are obviously easier to cope with than turned legs or those with a curve (such as sabre legs) or a taper.

If wood needs to be removed from part of a chair – wood that is wormy, wood that is badly damaged and cannot be renovated – the best way is to use a mortice chisel and straight edge. This type of chisel has a strong blade of equal width designed to cut across grain. Hit with a mallet. Make several cuts. Each should break away a wedge of wood. If not, slide the chisel along the chippings and slice free. Then cramp the rule and clean up the wood with a paring chisel.

The new piece should have a cut-in dovetail, and should be slightly larger than the old discarded part, so that it can be gradually perfected using the type of tool suitable for the wood – a plane for sturdy pieces, a sharp knife for thin inserts. Small gaps which may arise can be filled with wax. It is always important to make certain that the grain is

An example of basic low-cost Edwardian dovetailing. Earlier dovetailing would be less regular and there would be more dovetails.

running in the right direction. If part of the top rail needs replacing the old section needs to be taken out and a new section inserted, using dowels. This is a hazardous operation for those with limited woodworking ability unless the rail is very plain and symmetrical, for any renovations are plain to see. Many restorers put the replacement piece back in the rough unfinished state, and do the final shaping then. If there is likely to be any doubt about the shape of the rail, a photograph should be taken of the chair before any work is carried out. A Polaroid camera is invaluable for such purposes.

This kind of work – finishing it all off after the new piece has been securely fixed to the piece of furniture, whether it be chair, table, or whatever – can extend to the repair of a broken cabriole foot. This is an exceptionally vulnerable part of a chair, for the grain often runs from left to right, and it only needs a sharp knock for a chunk to chip off, often in a very neat fashion, as though lopped off by a chisel.

The first thing to do is to plane the surface of the break smooth, and make a good surface for glue. Using a cramp, glue on a block of wood, making certain to match the grain. Then using a range of suitable tools, such as a spokeshave, a sharp knife, or a chisel, carve and file the block to shape, finishing off with glasspaper.

Where there is a degree of upholstery, repairs can often be hidden, and metal plates, which can look clumsy in open chairs, can be used with freedom. Where there are loose arm and back joints, these can be glued and screwed without any need to disguise the screws. It is always important to take off any covers, even if there is a likelihood that the work can be carried out without disturbing them, for as you are working with glue there is always a chance of some of it getting on what might be valuable fabrics. When fixing metal plates it is advisable to drill holes into the wooden frame first, to stop the wood splitting. With both open and upholstered chairs, sofas, settees and stools, stout blocks of wood can be glued and screwed to the undersides of pieces of such furniture where major joints are loose, and it seems unnecessary to dismantle the chair and renew these joints.

Sometimes it is absolutely necessary to replace a mortice and tenon, the traditional woodworking joint, though there are many others, as can be seen from the accompanying illustrations (difficult to describe but crystal-clear in picture form). They all do the same job, though some are stronger than others.

If the hole is badly worn or wormy, cut away to sound wood and splice in a new piece of wood. If the tenon is broken cut off flush. Make a new tenon to fit into both facing pieces of wood. Cutting out a rectangle is more difficult than drilling to make space for a dowel, and in most cases a dowel will do the job. And of course the result of the above operation is not a 'real' mortice and tenon.

For extra strength, insert two dowels. As the new holes made in the wood will be hidden, it is vitally important that they are in alignment. To make certain of this, before any rectangles are chiselled out or holes drilled, insert two pins placed at strategic intervals into one wood face. Or nails with the heads clipped off can be used. Then place the two pieces of wood together, face to face, so that the protruding pins in the one piece of wood penetrate the other, thus giving a certain guide where to chisel or drill. This is far more functional than careful measuring with a rule.

Among the more annoying minor problems with carcase furniture is the sticking of drawers. The first thing to do is to look for obstructions, and where the rub marks are on the sides of the drawer, go over these with medium glasspaper. Rub down the top and bottom edges of the drawer with glasspaper wrapped round a cork block, or, as some prefer, folded into a pad. Rub a candle along the runners and sides. A drawer which 'jigs' may have a worn or missing guide inside the piece of furniture, and if this is the case glue in new strips of wood. If runners have worn unevenly it may be enough to fill in with plastic wood. Or the level can be raised by gluing on thin strips of wood, perhaps off-cuts of veneer. Failing that, it is no great task to replace. It will be easy to see where runners have been by differences in the colour or dirt level of the wood.

If a drawer goes too far in, the drawer stops have broken off. Cut small rectangles of wood and glue and nail them to the rail below the drawer so that the back of the drawer touches them when closed. If the drawer joints are loose, dismantle the drawer

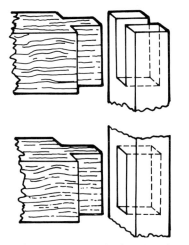

The housing joint in two versions, useful for sides.

Mortice and tenon joint and (above) a short cut.

The dovetail joint in its simplest form.

A tongued and grooved joint, seen in table tops.

The dowel is a useful multi-purpose device.
Normally, only one or two are needed, but when
extra strength is required three can be used.

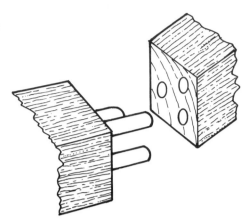

and reglue. This is not a major undertaking, and the most daunting task is to make certain that the drawer linings (sides) are not damaged when the dovetailing is exceptionally fine. Take out the bottom, removing screws, and it will slide out of grooves. Tap the joints apart and scrape off the glue. If the joints are slack tap in fine panel pins. If the bottom is twisted or warped replace with plywood, unless it is really good quality furniture. Twisted wood can be flattened by damping under heavy weights, and as drawer bottoms are often in two pieces one part may be all right and only the half-bottom may need attention.

If the drawer bottom is split, take it apart and glue it. This is easier than trying to glue the split together. If the drawers are 'lipped' it is not only a sign of quality but a vulnerable place, where chipping and damage is likely and it may be necessary to do a cosmetic repair, probably just using coloured wax.

Sometimes a drawer is locked, and it is the act of a vandal to try to open it with a crowbar or a stoutly wielded screwdriver. If it is not the top drawer which is locked, it may be possible to get at the lock from behind by taking out the drawers above, and unscrewing the lock, usually held in place by four screws. Sometimes dustboards prevent access, in which case it may be possible to take off the back of the piece of furniture. One drastic method is to cut a recess opposite the lock bolt from above and punch down, though this means a repair job when the drawer is finally opened, and a shoddy repair may be worse than a locked drawer. If it is a long drawer, the rail above may be forced upwards using cramps, so that the socket into which the bolt slots rides above the bolt. The obvious danger here is that the rail will crack. Of course, it is never wise to assume that because a drawer does not open it is locked. It may be merely an obstruction, something in the drawer jamming it solid, in which case the blade of a knife may well clear it.

A lock can be a work of art, and if it is working it adds to the value of whatever piece of furniture it is involved with. Although it is not by any means the most complicated mechanism made by man, in the sixteenth and seventeenth centuries, when much furniture was rude and functional, it was far more sophisticated than the piece it was protecting against thieves and light-fingered servants. So if a lock is removed from a drawer front on account of a missing key, take it off carefully, keeping the metal plates together if they become detached during the move, and resisting the temptation to have a quick peep. If no damage has been caused to the drawer front, and the lock can be replaced without any effort, it is worthwhile going to a locksmith to see if a key can

The underside of a piece of carcase furniture. Glued blocks often give strength to the structure and are unobtrusive.

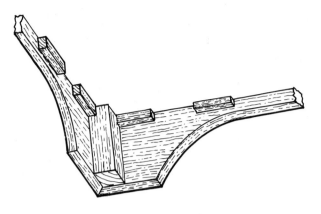

be cut. Many antiques dealers have a stock of miscellaneous keys, and may well sell the odd one, unless it is exceptionally picturesque and qualifies as a beautiful object in its own right.

If a lock appears to be jammed solid, and investigation seems sensible, and there is access to it, lie it on its face and carefully take off the back, not jigging it in any way for you may find that the works are often free-resting, without obvious attachments, only being held in place by the back-plate. If it seems to be a complicated lock – and many early locks were – make a drawing of where all the pieces fit. Any rust can be removed by a proprietary solvent as sold by the motor trade, and if oil is applied it should be thin, such as a sewing-machine oil. Where the lock is exceptionally delicate, graphite should be used as an oiling agent.

There are certain door locks which activate long rods which slot into holes at the top and bottom of the carcase. These are often fitted to high-quality furniture, and it will be frequently found that the lock is built into the wood, without exterior screws, and that access to it is virtually impossible without dismantling the entire piece of furniture.

Bent pieces on iron locks should be annealed before straightening out, and this can often be done with the lock intact. Annealing merely means softening, and makes metal easier to handle and less brittle. It is not a complicated process. The metal is heated to red heat with a blow-torch (butane blow-torches are today the most convenient) and then immersed in cold water. Brass should be allowed to cool slowly in the air.

Whatever is being treated should be surrounded by fireproof bricks, and the work should be carried out in a ventilated area, preferably in a dim light so that the operator can see when the metal reaches temperature, a glowing cherry red. Professionals use sulphuric acid (1 part acid: 6 parts water) but this can be hazardous to the amateur and occasional iron-worker.

Hinges may cause difficulties in such items of furniture as desks, bureaux, and gateleg and folding tables, as they will sometimes bind where the wood shrinks, warps, or expands. If this can be put right the hinges will work again. If not, the hinges may need to be moved, or replaced, though if it is a valuable piece of furniture a modern hinge will not add to the value and the awkward movement of a fall-front of a bureau or a leaf of a table may be preferable to a glaring anachronism. The fault might be simply that the screws fitting the hinge are too large, and are sticking up. Or even that round-headed screws instead of countersunk screws have been used. The large screws should be replaced by smaller screws or those of a more suitable nature, with the aperture plugged with a small piece of wood or a small piece of dowelling. If the hinge recess is too deep, pack with paper, card, or a piece of veneer; if it is too shallow, chisel out a sliver of wood.

Because of constant movement and a degree of pull, the wood around hinges sometimes splits and needs to be seen to, preferably not cosmetically, as plastic wood and other substitutes will not take the wear of real wood. Of all the items ever made where screws have a tendency to remain imbedded, the hinge is supreme, and because the screw top is usually flush with the hinge it is impossible to take it out using pincers or by chiselling away wood surrounding the top of the screw. If the slot is intact and not mangled, one method is to apply oil, and hold up to it a red-hot implement such as a nail held in a pair of pliers. An electric soldering-iron may be sufficient. If the screw is mangled the hinge may need to be drilled out, thus causing a certain amount of damage, and before this process is resorted to it is worthwhile trying to lever the hinge out using two spaced screwdrivers – two rather than one, to prevent the hinge buckling.

In all kinds of repairs and restoration the presence of old screws and nails can be a problem and a nuisance. When releasing a screw, the screwdriver should be exactly the right size, and a hard strike with a mallet may start it off. Grips on the shaft of the screwdriver may be a help. If all else fails, there is such a thing as a screw-remover, sometimes called a left-hand thread. The use of this involves drilling a hole through the centre of the screw, and screwing in the screw remover. So this is in a sense a screw within a screw. It is also possible to drill out a screw using a hollow cylindrical bit which takes out the screw with the wood immediately surrounding it. When this method is used, it means plugging the hole with a dowel section.

Fortunately nails are not much used in quality furniture, and in workaday furniture it may be acceptable to cut a depression round the head of the imbedded and unwanted nail, and pull out with pincers. A cylindrical bit as used with screws will also solve the problem. If joints will not part, even if struck smartly with a mallet, it may mean that there are not unseen screws or nails, but that the glue is holding up. Heat melts the old type of glue, but sometimes it is not possible to apply heat, in which case methylated spirits may work. Methylated spirits perishes old animal glues immediately, and this can be introduced through a small hole made with a drill. The glue can be heard breaking up as the methylated spirits acts upon it.

An easily remedied fault is a loose wooden knob on drawers or doors. Take it out, remove the old glue, and when replacing wrap a glue-saturated cloth round the dowel of the knob. If the knob is on veneer and not solid wood, and the veneer is more valuable than the knob, it is advisable to chip away at the shoulder of the knob so that when the knob is pulled out it will not pull the veneer with it. A knob which needs to be replaced or repaired and which is tight can be moved by gripping tightly, and turning one way and then the other.

If mouldings are broken, especially if they are integrated with the furniture they are adorning, these can be dowelled on in rough form, and then trimmed to match the surrounding or adjoining moulding, using any convenient tools, including home-made ones, such as doctored screwdrivers. Gouges can be very useful. Complicated mouldings can be made in more than one piece. To ascertain the section of such

Detail of Edwardian Pembroke table showing the kind of damage that occurs on the flaps.

A Regency rosewood and gilt-metal mounted library table of a type where repairs are often necessary, especially on the platform base where the weight of the pillar and heavy top are borne.

mouldings, drop a pack of cards over the existing length of moulding, placing the pack on its side, and trace the outline with pencil on paper. There is an ingenious device on the market which does the same task with movable lengths of metal, though for occasional repairs the pack-of-cards method may be acceptable – specialised tools and equipment are often quite expensive.

If the damaged moulding is on quality furniture, serious thought should be given to leaving it that way, or doing a cosmetic repair using wax, which can afterwards be coloured to match the surrounding wood, and which can be easily removed if too obtrusive. Antique furniture does not necessarily have to be brought up to showroom condition. For more ordinary furniture, it may be more sensible to replace damaged mouldings completely with bought-in replacement mouldings rather than spend hours doing something that is hardly worthwhile.

Tripod tables are often found in a damaged state. The legs are often slot-dovetailed in, resulting in a weakness. The strongest way to strengthen these is to fit metal plates, available ready-made from suppliers. These were often fitted when the tripod tables were new, so they are not anachronistic. If regluing is necessary, holding the tripod table together rigidly may be a problem, and you may need to improvise using a tourniquet. To avoid bruising furniture, sheets of foam are useful.

Table-tops sometimes split. Sometimes it is necessary to take the top off and close up under pressure, perhaps using the tourniquet technique. If there is a part split, insert a fillet of wood, perhaps a fragment of veneer (or two layers of veneer) used sideways, but if the split is too small this may be impossible. In which case, saw down the length of the crack, giving more room for a suitable wood insertion. The best type of saw to use for this type of problem is a fretsaw or a coping saw, because the split will probably have some slight curve if following the grain. The wood insert should preferably stand a little proud, and then be planed down so that it is flush with the surface. When polished it should be invisible.

Of course, splits don't occur without a reason, and in some way a split table-top is the result of stress. Sometimes it is impossible to work out why. Especially in round tables which have split across it may be necessary to do more than bring the two sections together and glue them under pressure (a good way to bring the two sections of a round table-top together is to rope them together). In this case, insert 'butterflies' of wood 2-3in (50-75mm) wide x 2½in (6mm) thick. Position the butterflies, scribe around them, cut recesses, using a mortice chisel across the grain. Clean up with a paring chisel. Release the cramps, add glue, cramp up with butterflies, weight them, but protect them with wax paper otherwise weights will stick to glue.

Round tables are often reinforced by a substantial batten screwed to the underside, and any repairs to the top will of course necessitate taking this piece off. Sometimes when the table is being reassembled it will be found that the screw holes won't line up. Rather than trying to replace the table-top in exactly the same position, with the possibility of part-plugging existing screw holes, it is better to turn the table slightly and drill new holes. The old screw holes will be hidden under the batten.

Sometimes a table-top will warp, and even if it is dampened under heat, and the warp seems to be cured, this is only temporary and when the table-top has dried out the fault will reappear. When the top has no framework, curvature can be countered by screwing one or more battens beneath. These battens may have to be substantial, and if the table is of value this method is a last resort. Where the leaf of a gateleg table has warped, a batten set at an angle can work, though it must be placed so that it clears the gate. Utilitarian tables, such as kitchen tables in pine, can be almost rebuilt without reduction in value, and warping in pine can often be cured in a few minutes by a few judiciously placed nails.

Among the traditional hard-worked tables where some damage is inevitable are draw-leaf tables, often of Victorian vintage with bulbous, often intricately-worked legs. The wind-up mechanism, used to open the two outer leaves so that the centre piece can be inserted is usually very substantial – though if it sticks it may need a drop of oil. Often the only problem is the absence of the wind-up handle, which is usually put somewhere safe (and thus gets lost). As no great pressure needs to be exerted, thin-nosed pliers can be used, or ring-spanners as used in the motor trade. These functional tables are not normally veneered, and as they are greatly undervalued and will eventually creep into the antique category, it is worthwhile bringing damaged and stained tops up to standard. The quality of the carving on the legs is often high, and any chips should be dealt with sympathetically. As there is no stress such repairs can be carried out using wax or plastic wood.

XXI

Handles

On early furniture, devices for pulling out drawers or opening doors were very basic, and in the sixteenth and seventeenth centuries these were of two main types: small wooden knobs usually decorated with fine lines and notching; and wrought iron pulls, in which a circular or triangular drop was suspended from a round or square back plate. The square back plate was often decorated along the edges with bevelled scrolls. These were made by blacksmiths, but by the middle of the seventeenth century the manufacture of drawer-pulls was becoming specialised, with the main centre in Birmingham.

With the coming of walnut, veneer, and marquetry something more elegant was demanded in the way of fittings, and although wooden knobs were still popular on country furniture, where it took a generation or more for new ideas to filter through, the trend in London and the centres of civilisation was for brass fittings. The model was made by a wood-carver, and a mould was made, into which molten brass was poured. Imperfections were filed off, and the final product was polished, sometimes lacquered and gilded. By the end of the seventeenth century the pear-shaped drop on a circular or star-shaped plate was universally applauded as the last word in elegance. The drop was fixed to the drawer by a narrow strip of brass passing through the woodwork and connected to the top of the drop. The ends of this brass strip, known as a tang, were separated, bent against the wood, and secured by small pins.

About 1710 came the loop, suspended from sockets at the heads of the bolts, and it was the most popular model for fifty years. There was a shaped backplate, through which two bolts passed through the woodwork, and they were secured at the back with screws. The early loops had shield-shaped backplates, sometimes ornate (with engraved birds, flowers, and scrolls), sometimes plain. Pierced backplates were very

117

An Edwardian reproduction George III card table with five finely tapered legs ending in spade feet. These legs, though elegant, are very vulnerable.

Opposite, above: An excellent example of a George I oak dresser base of the 1720s with appropriate drops for the handles. Other handles would look strange on this piece.
Below: A George II walnut chest of about 1745 with attractive brass handles. The question must be asked as to whether they are genuine or reproduction.

popular, but in the 1750s with the coming of mahogany the one-piece backplate made way for two circular 'roses' into which the loop slotted in at the bolt-heads. The loop became more elegant, assuming the shape of a swan's neck, a curve of beauty that was used for furniture pediments as well as decorative flourishes in the surface finish of furniture. However, the drop persisted throughout the eighteenth century, and this harked back to the much earlier furniture. The drops for Chippendale furniture were considerably heavier.

There were also asymmetrical rococo handles, fixed with screws or pins, or more usually nut and bolt, and the next step was to replace the circular roses, the loop hanging instead from a pair of bolts. One of the most radical developments was the ring hanging from a single bolt, and the backplates were oval, circular, and octagonal decorated in relief with the new motifs of the Neoclassical period – urns, laurel leaves, and formalised swags. Ormolu was now in use for high-quality furniture.

Until about 1780 these decorative accessories were traditionally made, but a Birmingham firm patented the stamping out in sheet metal of decorations, ornaments and devices for cabinet furniture. These have proved vulnerable to the passing of the years, and are often found with splits and dents, though fortunately brass is a fairly malleable metal and if the backplates are taken off the parent furniture they can be repaired from behind, any splits closed up by a careful but persistent hammering of the surrounding metal or by soldering, and the dents knocked out.

Brass handles were ideal for mahogany, but they looked trivial on some heavy furniture, and as furniture styles were beginning to change drastically it was time to return to the knob, made in many materials including brass, wood, and ivory. The brass knobs were quite small, and often had serrated edges with embossed motifs. Ivory was much used for small drawers, sometimes stained green. Wooden knobs were often inlaid with mother-of-pearl at the centres, and grooved. Porcelain knobs were also used for feminine pieces of furniture. Knobs became larger and more intrusive, and the brass fittings on eighteenth-century furniture were often replaced with knobs that were completely out of character. The knobs were either dowelled in, and rounded off with wooden buttons, or screwed in. It is easy to tell when knobs have replaced brass fittings by looking for the old screw holes, though these may be hidden by the base of the knob.

Of course, anachronistic knobs can be replaced by reproduction brass loops or drops, which may need to be lacquered or modestly distressed to tone them down, though the quality of many reproduction fittings is very high. But there is no point in replacing knobs which could be contemporary with the furniture.

Towards the end of the nineteenth century other metals such as pewter and copper were used for furniture accessories, and many of the practitioners in the Arts and Crafts movement favoured heavy iron fittings, especially hinges and locks. Some of the iron handles designed for no-nonsense progressive oak furniture were more suitable for front doors.

There was also the first sign of a radical new approach to the whole question of opening doors and drawers – the shaped single block: first in wood, and eventually in a wide variety of new materials such as Bakelite and later plastics, chrome, and exotic natural substances such as onyx. The handles of Art Deco furniture were often curious and ingenious, and became engineering devices rather than furniture fittings.

Other fittings associated with furniture include escutcheons and all kinds of trims

A George III mahogany kneehole desk. Are the handles original? It may appear so. But why is there a curious circular mark on the left of the lefthand drawer? Has someone contemplated fitting bun knobs?

to make key-holes more elegant. Sometimes the surrounds of key-holes are missing. This is especially true of work boxes and writing boxes which have had a good deal of steady wear over the years, and it is a simple operation replacing them, though it is a good idea to look around, in antique shops and in books, so that any replacement material is not out of character. Ivory was often used, and this can be cut with a sharp knife, with the key-hole drilled out and then shaped with a fret saw (which of course can be threaded through the hole that the drill makes). As ivory has a grain, and therefore can split, sticky brown tape should be applied to the back. Celluloid makes a passable substitute for ivory. There are no problems in sticking ivory to the wooden base. Scotch glue with a little garlic added can be used, as well as modern contact adhesives and other glues. The underside of the ivory or similar material should be scored to give a tooth. Any old glue or dirt in the recess should of course be removed. As ivory, unlike wood, cannot be planed level, the recess should be the right depth, and it may be necessary to deepen it or insert a fillet of wood, such as a fragment of veneer.

A fine Davenport of about 1870 with a leather-inset writing surface. If the leather is stained it is better to try to remove the stain than to re-leather, and, in fact, vestiges of stains in no way detract from the general appearance or value of the piece.

122

XXII

Leather

The main uses of leather in the manufacture of furniture are in upholstery, in the manufacture of trunks and chests, and in the provision of tops for writing tables and desks, in which a light leather is employed. These tops often need to be relaid, though if there are ugly ink-stains but otherwise the surface seems to be holding up, it is worthwhile trying to get rid of these stains using a solution of oxalic acid crystals in water (¼tsp (6ml) into a ¼pt (125ml) of warm water). Or, if this fails to work, domestic bleach applied to the stain only, and rinsed off quickly. A hole in the leather can be repaired by gluing on a patch of thin leather to the underside – if it can be reached. A hole indicates some deterioration, and it is possible that when an attempt is made to remove the leather intact there may be tearing.

If the leather has become unglued where it abuts the wooden surround, pull back to as far as it will go, gently tugging, and rub down the wood underneath with glasspaper, either in the form of a pad or, if there is room, wrapped round a wooden block. If the reverse of the leather has become shiny or matted through the infiltration of dirt, spirit soap can be used, or it can be gently scored with a knife to give a tooth when it is pasted down again.

The adhesive generally used for laying down leather tops is paperhanger's paste, either in powder or paste form. It has to be twice as thick as the manufacturers state in their instructions. Polyvinyl acetate emulsion is also acceptable, but do not use too much as it may come through. If the entire top is to be replaced, a knife blade is the most efficient, and all old paste and stubborn patches of leather should be removed. Cut a piece of leather slightly larger than the area to be covered for leather shrinks when the adhesive dries. Lay the leather down, pressing out the bubbles and wrinkles, and press the sides into the border recesses with the thumb nail. Any surplus leather should be trimmed off with a sharp knife and a straight edge.

Ready-made tops are often decorated with a border and ornamental flourishes, but a border can be made using a tooling wheel. These can provide a plain or ornamental border. The wheel should be heated in a flame, then wiped with a clean rag to which a little methylated spirit has been added. Using a straight edge, the wheel is impressed into the leather, though it is a good idea to mark the leather out beforehand, perhaps using a pastel pencil which will not leave a permanent mark, for leather is not cheap and there is only one chance of doing it correctly.

A more elaborate kind of tooling uses gold leaf, in strip form with a thin paper backing. The wheel is heated, and the gold leaf is pressed onto the leather with the tooling wheel. Any surplus gold is brushed off with a sable brush. The gold leaf does not usually need any adhesive, but if it seems reluctant to stick, egg white can be used. For those with a taste of adventure, decorative touches can be added using the tooling wheel in association with stencils or 'French curves', transparent plastic templates sold by art shops and retailers of drawing-office equipment.

Leather tops should be cleaned with spirit soap and white spirit, and varnished, if need be, with shellac dissolved in methylated spirit – a kind of French polish. This process can be reversed by the application of methylated spirits. If the leather has been

This chair from 1926 is covered with leather, always a prestigious material, and it is interesting to note that chairs covered with other materials are often half the price.

A rosewood Davenport of about 1860. The leather top is bubbled. Should it be put right? This is always a difficult decision.

124

patched, varnishing will help to blend in the old leather and the new. Leather tops can be waxed using microcrystalline wax.

Leather can be treated in a variety of ways – dyeing, staining, plating (producing a shiny finish), embossing, painting, enamelling (which gives patent leather as used in shoes and not much employed in furniture leather) and scraping, resulting in suede. Initially it is tanned, the most common method using tannin, a natural substance from vegetable matter. Old leather should be 'fed'; there is an excellent old-established dressing from Probert's. Old leather can be brittle, and if in a bad condition can be pulled apart exactly like thick cardboard. A sure sign of trouble is the leather turning pink, especially on the reverse (flesh) side, and the deeper the red the worse it is. This is known as red rot, and if caught in time may be treatable with a potassium lactate; if advanced the leather can be impregnated with acrylic resin in trichloroethane, 1 part to 3. All treatment is from the reverse side.

In early furniture leather was stretched across the framework of the chair and affixed with brass-headed studs, and the holes made in the leather are very vulnerable. If it is a valuable chair, as it is likely to be, and the leather is passable and not likely to come apart when sat upon or when leaned on if the backing is leather, the best course is probably to leave matters as they are, for in prising out the studs a good deal of damage can be caused. As with desk tops, heavyweight leather can be cleaned with a mild solution (2 parts to 100) of spirit soap in white spirit, and rinsed off with white spirit. Suede should be cleaned with a granular cleaner sold for this express purpose.

Hide, often with the hair still attached, was used for chests and trunks, sometimes well-studded, and often these studs are holding the leather together without this being immediately obvious, and corroded studs which cry out for replacement should be removed, if at all, with great circumspection, and a cosmetic operation might be preferable. Any leather that is attached to canvas and wood will very likely split apart if any attempt is made to separate them. As with desk-top leather, fragile leather can be patched from the back, especially if there is cracking but as yet no splitting. It is tempting to tart up gilded decoration that has faded badly, but it is better to leave this alone as restoration work of this type is usually ill directed.

This could easily be taken as a Spanish leather-seated and leather-backed chair of some antiquity, but it is in fact an 1870 piece. The leather is unsupported, and no matter how many studs are put in there is always a risk of the leather splitting.

125

A Victorian library table from the 1850s or perhaps a trifle later with a green leather top with key pattern border. It would be rare if this were not a replacement.

XXIII

Metals

Furniture, of course, does not necessarily consist of just wood, and sometimes, as in the ormolu of French furniture, other materials are very important. In some cases they deteriorate more than the wood, and are often more vulnerable.

Brass has probably been used to decorate furniture more than any other material. It is composed of 65 per cent copper and 35 per cent zinc, and if possible when being cleaned it should be removed from the furniture in case the chemicals damage the wood, or, more likely, the finish. An ammonia solution, taking care not to breathe in the fumes, will remove dirt and grease, and after rinsing, a solution of oxalic acid – or vinegar, which is safer – should be applied in the proportions of 2tbsp (230ml) of vinegar: 1tbsp (115ml) of salt in 1pt (560ml) of water. Rinse thoroughly and polish with oil or Brasso. Corroded brass needs to be washed in a moderately strong warm solution of washing soda, and the corrosion should come away by wiping or a brisk brushing. If not, the surface may need to be worked with steel wool. The scratches can be taken out with jewellers' rouge, an abrasive red powder, which can be used dry or made into a paste.

Holes or cracks in brass can be filled with resin mixed with very fine brass filings or solder, afterwards coloured. Hollow brass, as used in some drawer knobs and door knobs, can easily get damaged. The usual place where a knob breaks is around the waist, between the front part and the back. Araldite can also be used. The two parts of the knob should be kept together with adhesive tape until the adhesive has set.

Brass is sometimes lacquered, and it is often worth taking this protective coating off if it seems grimy. Afterall, it can always be reapplied if on second thoughts the brass looks 'wrong' without it.

Brass was often used in eighteenth and nineteenth century furniture as inlay and stringing, and there are often problems when the wood in which it is set shrinks or twists in any way, in which case the inlay buckles up, if stringing, in the form of a shallow loop. Do not pull it to lift it off, but try to prise it out with a tiny wedge of wood. If the base has shrunk it may be sufficient to cut a piece out and relay the brass. If the brass stringing has lifted it may be enough to cut with a fine hacksaw, snip off a tiny length, and press down. Although the stringing will now be in two parts this will

A George II mahogany wine cooler on stand with handsome brass fitments. It is a matter of choice whether the brass should be brightened up, lacquered, or subdued, and there is no one easy answer. In the end it depends on the preference of the owner.

not show. Woodworking glue will not work very readily with brass, and a modern adhesive should be used. As brass is springy, it should be cramped down while the adhesive is setting. Brass inlay can be kept in place with pins, the heads being nipped off and rubbed down with glasspaper. It is advisable to drill small holes first so that the wood beneath does not split.

Fretted brass as used on the galleries of desks or in Regency and Victorian carcase furniture is often found to have bits missing, and to replace these take a pattern of the existing part, using heel ball, a pencil, or tracing paper. It is often easier to remove the fretted brass first from its mounting. The replaced pieces can be cut from thinner brass sheet than the existing type, and soldered on. If the fretting is very badly damaged it may be possible to take out pieces so that what is left is symmetrical, even if a new design.

There are two kinds of soldering: hard and soft. Soft soldering is not so strong as hard soldering, but it is much easier to work with. Using an electrical soldering iron presents few difficulties, as the flux and solder are combined usually in wire form and they don't need to be applied separately. Good soldering depends on the surfaces to be joined being absolutely dirt and grease free, so that the metal gleams and provides good surfaces. Solder-paint is a flux and solder which is painted on, and then subjected to the soldering iron.

Bronze, an alloy of copper and tin in various proportions, acquires a patina, which comes in a variety of blue and greeny colours, and is often much prized, especially on statues and other decorative items. If you want to remove patina, flake or scrape it off with a wire brush. A 10 per cent solution of acetic acid in water will remove odd bits, but leave a reddish colour, which can be rubbed off. Wash off this solution with water. Should it be wanted, an acceptable patina can be produced by using a dilute solution of salt and copper nitrate, followed by immersion in 5 parts ammonium chloride, 1 part of oxalic acid, all in 100 parts of weak vinegar, and kept there several days. Whether it is desirable on aesthetic grounds to fabricate a patina on bronze fittings which will almost certainly be contemporary with the furniture with which they are associated is doubtful; a good wash with water may well be enough. If the bronze is suffering from corrosion, and is flaking, it might be advisable not to clean it off, especially if the bronze is very decorative (as it is likely to be), but to fix it with lacquer.

Iron and steel accessories and fitments are not so often found in furniture except in the form of hinges and locks or the bands on chests and coffers, and although signs of age on old iron items are inevitable it may be advisable, if the object is of value, to arrest deterioration by the application of Vaseline. Surface rust, removable by a fine abrasive of your choice, may turn out to be more serious than at first supposed, and any restoration should be carried out with circumspection. Where the object is utilitarian, or where iron brackets have been used to repair or reinforce shaky joints, a car rust-remover can be used. Holes caused by rust can be filled by acrylic resin and iron filings, or one of the plastic metals, suitably tinted.

Ormolu, from the French *or moulu* (ground gold), was known to the Egyptians and the Romans, and was widely used in eighteenth-century France and to a lesser extent England. True ormolu is gold applied in an amalgam of mercury onto bronze or brass. The mercury is driven off in poisonous fumes by the application of heat, and the process was so dangerous that in the nineteenth century it was made illegal in England,

A nineteenth-century étagère. The mounts could be of inferior material with thin gilding, and the owner must be very wary of doing anything dramatic. As the piece is high quality it is likely that the mounts are of good quality too.

where it was replaced by electro-gilding and dipping, although it continued to be used on the continent. In old ormolu, the areas in relief were burnished, but otherwise the surface was matt. In second-quality ormolu there was no gilding, just burnishing and the application of gold lacquer.

Sometimes the metal beneath the lacquer becomes tarnished, and it needs to be rubbed down and re-lacquered. Old lacquer can be removed with acetone. To regild, the best and most authentic way is the use of gold leaf. The surface of the metal must be absolutely clean, wiped over with a weak solution of ammonia, then dried. An even coat of gold size (a weak glue from boiled linseed oil and ochre) is applied. There are two kinds of gold size: one dries in 2-4hr, the other in 8-12hr. When the surface is

A French mahogany table of about 1880 with a brass gallery. Brass grille-work should always be closely inspected, though repairs, using existing sections as a pattern, are not difficult.

Opposite, above: Being an 1870 French card table, it is possible that the metal mounts are not of the quality of those on earlier pieces, and any refurbishing should be done with caution.
Below: Locks on old chests are often missing, and rather than try to replace the ironwork it is often better to leave well alone.

slightly tacky, it is ready for the pieces of gold leaf, which should be placed gently on the size, slightly overlapping and pointing the same way. When the surface is covered, take a cotton cloth and rub over, blending the gold leaves together to present an unbroken surface.

The new gilding can be made to match old gilding by rubbing very gently with fine glasspaper, or by applying watercolour washes. The newly laid ormolu can be sealed with an alcohol varnish, but never a turpentine-based varnish.

However, it may be sufficient to wash the ormolu with soap and water, or, if bad, a mild solution of ammonia and water, as with brass, or the application of ammonia with a brush. Another cleaning method uses 1oz (29g) of sodium hydroxide and 85g (3oz) of sodium potassium tartrate in 1 quart (1.14 litre) of distilled water. When this has been applied, rinse under running water. Never use metal polish on ormolu as this will remove the gold.

Brass was often juxtaposed with ormolu, and it is important to recognise the difference as brass will take a good deal more rough and ready refurbishment. Some of the best English ormolu was made in the Soho factory of Matthew Boulton between 1762 and 1776. The best ormolu was cast, but about 1800, cheap mechanical pressings came in, which were lightweight and insubstantial, and in the 1830s and 1840s spelter (zinc) and Britannia metal were used to imitate true ormolu. This must be borne in mind when dealing with ormolu, and finding that the metal is not brass but grey and anonymous. If this happens, there is no point in spending time and money regilding the gold leaf.

Pewter is not often regarded as a component of furniture, but during the last few years of the nineteenth century and the beginning of the twentieth it was used as inlay and for adornment, sometimes in the form of motifs, sometimes as panels. Although pewter started as a cheap substitute for silver, used for plates and drinking vessels, there was no pretence at it being anything else when used in Art Nouveau furniture. There is no point in it being highly polished; that would be quite out of character.

As it is a soft metal, pewter can be damaged quite easily, but as pewter was often hammered to make a decorative dimpled effect, it is possible to redistribute any damaged metal by hammering, using the round head of an ordinary hammer. However, it may be necessary to remove the pewter from the furniture and place it over a suitable piece of wood or a sandbag before beginning work. Pewter was usually tacked on to furniture, and some damage is likely to occur around the nails, making the panels or motifs loose. Hammering the nail holes until they almost disappear will solve this minor problem.

Pewter should be washed with soap and water, thoroughly rinsed and dried off, and perhaps coated with Vaseline. Small stains can be removed with a mild abrasive, but it is wise not to rub too strenuously. Corrosion should be treated by soaking in paraffin. Broken pewter can be mended with epoxy resin adhesive (though it is difficult to match the distinctive colour and texture of the metal) and it can be soldered, though care should be taken if one decides to use this method as the melting point of this alloy is low.

XXIV

Rushing and Caning

Sometimes country chairs are bought with which something appears to be vaguely wrong. They are often old ladder-back chairs, or stick-backs. It will soon be seen that the trouble lies in the seat, wooden, well-fitted, but not quite right. A little investigation from the underside will reveal the truth: the chair has been reseated, probably because the original seat was caned or had been made using rushes. Where rushes grow, as in ancient Egypt, they have been used for domestic purposes, and like weaving and knitting, rushwork has existed almost unchanged for thousands of years.

A dry atmosphere is bad for rush seats, and after about twenty years the rushes begin to sag, and if not dealt with they begin to fray and break up. If that happens the chair needs rerushing, or, as so often happens, a replacement is sought in wood. If not too far gone, the chair should be taken outside and sprayed with water, and with a bit of luck the spring will return to them. If not, rerushing is not a complicated procedure and, with the aid of a few books, it is an easily-learned skill. It is equally likely that the rushes are mildewed and rotten, and there is no remedy for rushes in this state. Rushing is a craft that has been enjoying a revival over the last few years, and craft suppliers will either be able to let you have some – about two pounds in weight for the average chair – or will be able to suggest a source.

The rushes are soaked in cold water for ten minutes, taken out, and placed under a cloth to keep the moisture in for twenty-four hours. The next step is to strip remnants of old rush from the frame of the seat. This does not involve taking out tiresome tacks or nails, because rushes are wound over the frame. Rushes are used singly or in twos, twisted together. The rush is laid over the left-hand side of the front bar of the frame, held firmly against the inside of this front bar, then twisted hard. Pass the longer length of rush under the frame, up and around the left-hand front bar, thus holding fast the short end which is now anchored. The long length is then taken across the front of the frame, passed around the right-hand front bar, behind the length you have just pulled across. Pass the length over the front right-hand bar, keeping close to the corner, and taking it under and across the frame to (viewing from above) the top right-hand corner, and so on to the top left-hand corner. Proceed until the frame is filled. There are many variations in rushing, but once the principle has been grasped the process can be made as simple or as complex as the user wishes. The main thing is to get the initial strand firmly anchored.

Probably you will run out of rush lengths fairly soon; you merely join them together to continue. The reef-knot is best (right over left, right under left); this tightens as it is pulled. As you work inwards you will find that there is a gap between the rushes going over the bar and those going under on each of the four sides. This gap must be packed, with short or broken lengths, and rammed home with a wedge-shaped piece of wood. This packing stops the rows of rushes from slipping, and also provides strengthening at the most vulnerable points.

On completion the end of the final rush is knotted to one of the rushes on the bottom layer, then tucked away out of sight to clean up the operation.

As with rush-seated chairs, many caned chairs have had their seats replaced. It is very easy to tell when a chair was once caned, as the frame of the seat will have a sequence of holes in them where the cane was threaded through. The quality of cane-seated and backed chairs is likely to be higher than that of rush-seated chairs, though during the second half of the nineteenth century the practitioners of the Arts and Crafts movement were anxious to revitalise rushwork and produced some designs which now fetch high prices at auction.

The use of caning for chairs and settees was introduced in the 1660s, and reached a high point with the bergère suite. Split rattan canes were used to make an interleaved mesh. There was a slight give to make the furniture more comfortable than wood.

The first question to ask is whether the chair warrants time and money spent on it and whether the replacement seat is acceptable. If just a few canes are broken it may be possible to remove these and replace with fresh canes, stained to match those in place. Unravelled canes can be pushed back into position, and stuck with waterproof adhesive. As with rushes, suitable cane can be bought from craft shops, and is easier to get hold of as the practice of recaning is more popular than rerushing. The chair frame should be thoroughly cleaned, and old fragments of cane poked out of the holes. The holes should be cleared of all obstructions, perhaps by using a gimlet or a small screwdriver.

Although this gilt bergère chair is not so old as it looks (it is of 1900 vintage) the quality of the caning is so good that any repairs would have to be in keeping and would be expensive if done professionally.

A pair of William and Mary walnut chairs of about 1690 with caning of high quality. If damaged, this caning would be difficult to replace in period except by a qualified practitioner of the art.

The cane should be soaked in cold water for several hours to make it workable, and then a length of cane should be drawn through the centre hole in the back of the frame for half its length, then taken up through the next hole to the left. Both ends should be taken to the corresponding holes in the front. Unlike rushwork, one end of the cane in front is wedged with a tapered plug, while the other is threaded along the underside, up through the next hole, and across to the far end of the seat. Threading cane is common sense. Anyone who has threaded laces into shoes will have no problems. The canes should be kept parallel and not pulled too hard, for they will tighten up as the work proceeds. The smooth side of the cane should be on top. As you carry on, you use a moveable plug for each hole to keep the cane reasonably taut.

The new strand is secured by winding it twice round the cane running between the holes on the underside, and pulled tight. When the left-hand side of the seat is done, unplug, and do the same for the right. The procedure for caning left to right is the same, on top of the up and down canes. Then do another set, this time interleaving the cane with the up and down canes. You now have a mesh comprised of small squares.

The holes in all four corners are free; they have not been used in the up and down and left and right weaving operation. The next stage is to provide diagonal caning, interleaving under the left to right strands, over the up and down strands, starting from the corners. That is one diagonal; for the other, reverse the interleaving, over the left to right canes, under the up and down canes. A border can be provided, though structurally not necessary, by running a cane between the holes, using the caning in position to hold it fast.

Professional recaning is expensive, and an ordinary humdrum chair can cost more to recane than it is worth. A sensible course is to proceed methodically, making certain that your under and over threading of the canes is systematic. If not, you will have a sagging section, and will have to start over again for that particular stage. Some of these procedures will be useful when dealing with wickerwork furniture. The structure of all such furniture is obvious, and it will be readily apparent how it was made, so it is usually a simple question of refurbishing damaged elements, perhaps interweaving replacements, staining if the new material is too stark, and using household bleach to tone down if the colour is too strong.

XXV

Upholstery

There are two basic types of upholstery, 'stuff-over' and 'drop-in' or loose seats. The latter is much easier to do, as it mostly involves replacing the existing material or any padding with a modern equivalent, though with the present attention on foam and its fire risk it might be more comforting to refurbish the existing padding. A drop-in seat may or may not be webbed, but if it is there won't be the miles of spiral spring which in upholstered chairs and settees press down with considerable force on the webbing, eventually leading to problems.

When the webbing of such an upholstered chair is sagging or broken it can be satisfactorily tackled from beneath. The webbing will be covered by a piece of hessian, probably frayed, and easily torn away, leaving the tack heads proud and quickly removable with a pair of pincers, rather than gouging them out with a screwdriver. The springs will be attached to the existing webbing with twine, and it is a good idea to see how this is done in case the webbing needs renewing. Sometimes the springs have simply come adrift, and need re-attaching to the webbing. The needle used is half-circular; four knots are used for each spring, spaced evenly in a circle, so if one knot, or even two knots, break the spring will still hold.

136

An upholsterer's nightmare!

If the springs are pushing upwards into the seat, making it uncomfortable or lumpy, this is more of a problem, and as the chair or settee may need stripping down it may be a job for a professional. There are so many people doing upholstery as a hobby and to earn pin-money that even a strenuous reupholstery job can be surprisingly cheap.

Traditional webbing is made from flax, cotton or jute, and is very durable. A modern substitute is rubber webbing, and whether this is used or not depends on the desire for a springy feeling or authenticity. If you are re-webbing look at the pattern of the previous webbing, and repeat it. It will be over-and-under, and each length of webbing is tacked firmly at each end, not with just one tack, but several in a row or perhaps a double row. The main object is to get the webbing tense; this can be done with a block of wood, with a 'V'-cut in it. The webbing is strained across the top of this block, with the 'V' resting on the angle of the wooden frame. When you have tacked

In common or garden furniture such as this, is reupholstery worthwhile, or would it be better to go to a second-hand warehouse and replace it?

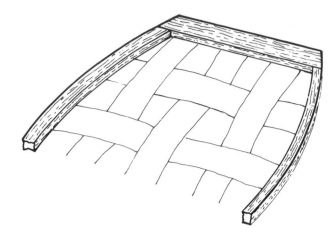

The underside of a chair showing the over-and-under method of applying webbing.

A George III mahogany rail-back chair of around 1790. The seats are stuffed and covered with gold dralon. Some would find this a tolerable substitute for velvet, but if one is paying more than £500 a chair others would not.

138

down the length of webbing, leave a little bit extra, turn back, and tack down. There is no pressure on these and a couple of tacks will do. There are specialist tools associated with reupholstery, and if several chairs are being dealt with it is worth making enquiries. Do not use silly little tacks when hammering in. Never retie the springs until the webbing is in place, stretched, and firm. When all is complete, replace or renew the hessian cover. This does nothing but keep out of the dust – not very successfully.

If you are doing anything with the padding you may find that the existing material is horsehair or flock. Neither of them will cause your house to burn down in five minutes flat. Horsehair is now in demand by upholsterers, and if you decide to discard existing horsehair in the furniture you are doing up, do not throw it away. Foam is much easier to fit in, of course, and is not so dusty or messy. It can be cut with a pair of dampened scissors, and trimmed off to the exact size. The choice of filling is up to the repairer, as is the covering, which should be cut larger than the seat area so that it presses down

A rather gruesome padoukwood reproduction chair of about 1900 with drop-in seats (of hide). Sometimes inappropriate upholstery can indicate a shifty ancestry.

139

over the seat, leaving sufficient for it to be tacked to the underframe of the chair. All unsightly edges are covered with braid or similar.

The covering fabric should be put on methodically, laid carefully on top of the seat so that the overlap is even. The first tack is then driven in not too far in the centre-front rail, then the centre-back, then the sides. This will stabilise the cover; then, smoothing the material towards the strike, continue hammering in tacks, keeping up the tension in the material and being very careful if the material is fragile or easily separates into strands. Spare material can be snipped off, and a 'V' cut in for the back. For drop-in seats a double pleat is needed for the corners, in stuff-over seats a single pleat is sufficient. Any material can be used for a stuff-over chair, but for drop-in seats it has to be similar in thickness to the original so that it will fit comfortably, not jut up or wobble about.

If there are loose arm or back joints in upholstered furniture it may be necessary to strip off the cover to get at the fault. You may want to replace the fabric, so as you take out tacks remember *where* they go, and if the material is folded or pinched, remember *how*. A joint which is out of sight is a joint which can be robustly repaired in the simplest manner, with a rough block of wood, sturdy screws, metal plates, or a good helping of glue.

Of course, as in everything, there are short cuts. Replacing webbing can be dusty. It can take time, and tying the springs to the webbing can be fiddly, especially if a half-circular needle is not to be found, even in the do-it-yourself enthusiast's tin of screws and nails. Turn the offending piece of furniture upside down, and take a pattern of the underside of the frame using a large piece of card or paper. Trace this shape on plywood, and cut out with a fretsaw or an electric saw. Then firmly fix the plywood on the base, using long screws, so that they hold the springs as effectively as any webbing. Drill holes in the plywood first, to reduce any chance of it splitting.

If the material covering an old chair is contemporary with the chair itself, take advice before recovering. The material may be worth far more than the chair itself.

XXVI

Veneer

One of the problems met with in repairing and renovating antique furniture is damaged veneer. Old veneer is thicker than modern machine-cut veneer, and if the veneer is of the thickness of a 5p piece it is probably genuine antique, and this must be borne in mind when applying shop-bought veneers. Some woods have become unobtainable, and if rare veneers need replacement, the possibility of fresh supplies not being available may mean that to achieve the desired results a veneer of similar graining and figure may have to be stained.

'Standard' veneers such as mahogany are easily obtainable from specialist suppliers, but for small quantities it is possible to find replacements in marquetry kits, sold by craft shops. It has long been the practice of professional restorers to rummage through junk shops and such outlets looking for badly damaged furniture to cannibalise, just for the sake of the wood and veneer. When Edwardian furniture was less popular than it is today supplies were no problem, nor was there any difficulty in stripping the veneer from its carcase. It is now a long time since Victorian furniture was seen as raw material for salvaging wood or veneer. There are now many firms which provide old wood for do-it-yourself enthusiasts and the trade, and these should be visited at regular intervals. Recently the author bought an 8ft (2.44m) length of mahogany, approximately 6in (38cm) square for £4. For small quantities, look around in junk shops, jumble sales or boot sales. Old school rulers, of no value at all, are made of boxwood, much used for inlay and stringing. Round rulers, formerly used in offices and especially by accountants, are made of ebony.

Veneer can either rely for its effect on its figure or graining, or can be presented in the form of a picture (marquetry) or an arrangement of geometric shapes (parquetry). Often several pieces from the same piece can be displayed in a 'mirror' fashion. The question might be asked: why use veneer? Some woods were very expensive even in the eighteenth and nineteenth centuries, far too dear to use in the solid; additionally, some of the most attractive exotic woods had a tendency to twist and turn and therefore, even if money was no object, were unsuited to working in the solid.

Before replacing damaged veneer, the whole operation should be carefully appraised. If a defect can be put right, it is far better to do this, as a replacement veneer does detract from the value of an antique piece no matter how carefully it is applied.

An old method of removing an entire sheet of veneer was to lay the veneered surface down for a few days in long grass; another is to place the veneer against a quantity of damp sawdust. One restorer soaked off veneer in his bath! For a quick job, use a damp cloth and controlled heat from a domestic iron.

Inlay covers not only the top but the frieze and the legs on this curious Victorian table. If there is damage is repair warranted?

A Victorian credenza with so much veneer that any damage involves a major repair job.

One of the main problems with old veneer is bubbling, when the veneer rises from the carcase like a shallow dome. Sometimes the bubble can be removed by puncturing. Drill two holes, and inject glue, using a hypodermic syringe. Apply pressure. Some restorers drill holes and inject from the underside, to prevent any damage to the veneer, but when the bubble is pressed down it is not likely that the holes will be noticed. If the work is being carried out away from the edge use a pad of softwood, held down by a cramped beam, placed so that the pressure is even.

The best kind of glue to use is Scotch glue, not only for veneers but for all furniture repairs. (A viable alternative is polyvinyl acetate PVA.) Though more messy than modern glues, Scotch glue has the advantage that is it right for the job, that it was most likely the kind of glue that was used in the first place, and that, in the future, if further repairs need to be carried out, it can be removed just as easily as the old glue you may be getting rid of now. It comes in 'pearls'. Two handfuls should be put in a shallow container (perhaps plastic, though some restorers use a tin can), covered with cold water, and allowed to soak overnight.

This container should be placed in another container, three-quarters full of water, brought to the boil and allowed to simmer. After about half an hour there will be wisps of steam when stirred, and a scum will form, which should be removed, using, for

An example of marquetry of the highest quality.

example, a piece of flat wood. The glue should be creamy, without lumps, but it should not be loose enough to allow droplets to drip, nor should it be like toffee. The main requirement is that it is workable, and it must always be remembered that away from heat it solidifies very rapidly. To thin the glue down, add hot water; to thicken it, add more pearls. For use with veneer the glue can have a thinner consistency than if you are joining joints together.

If the bubble on the veneer will not respond to treatment, or if it is broken, cut with a sharp knife, and open further, removing old glue and grime, then apply fresh glue and pressure. An electric soldering iron will melt the vestiges of ancient glue, making it easy to remove. Some veneers, such as walnut, especially oyster (where the veneer is made up of cross-lengths from a branch), are more inclined to break up on account of their tight intricate figuring, and there may be sections which are

impossible to renovate and need to be replaced. When replacing veneer, the colour should be lighter rather than darker, as wood can always be stained to match.

But what is the right colour? A drop of methylated spirits on the veneer will give an indication, though a good rub down will give double assurance as this will take off any discolouring surface treatment, such as varnish or wax. Some of these treatments can stop heat penetrating the wood, so when the use of a hot iron for some reason fails to work it may be that the polish or varnish needs to be removed.

As far as possible, the grain and figure should be followed. If it is a small area to be taken out, use a boat shape for interior repairs, a wedge for edges, and cut with a very sharp knife, such as a Stanley knife or a scalpel, at an angle so that there is a bevel. The replacement veneer should be a trifle on the large side, so that it can be trimmed to be exact. The place where the veneer has been taken out should be cleaned thoroughly of old glue and grime. If the replacement veneer is just a fraction 'proud' it may be possible to bow the patch upwards so that it can be forced in.

Sometimes the old patch comes out easily, sometimes the glue holds it fast. Hot linseed oil will help speed the process, allowing time for it to sink in, and a hot household iron should be applied, with a clean slightly dampened cloth between the wood and the iron, as in removing entire veneers. Heat in short bursts of five to ten seconds, and any darkening of the wood resulting from the heat will soon disappear. To apply the new patch use the round head of a hammer, which has just been immersed in hot water, to press the veneer down. The hammer head should be held with both hands, and the warmth and pressure should prevent the glue from setting. If the glue does set, despite precautions, keep the iron and the dampened cloth handy. During the glue-setting time, a matter of five to ten minutes, the wood should be secured by veneer nails.

When replacing missing pieces of veneer, gum down the existing sections so that you will have a good surface to work with. It is a good idea to roughen the back of replacement patches and pieces, using the teeth of a tenon saw blade held in a vice.

Replacing veneer which is functional, relying for its effect on grain and figure, is much easier than repairing marquetry where a picture may need to be restored. And this picture may be more complicated than at first appears. If a section of marquetry needs to be taken out, first of all make a tracing, and ensure that the different woods are clearly marked or coded. This tracing can be transferred to the new veneer or veneers using carbon paper, or the tracing can be neatly cut up, and the marked pieces glued directly onto the veneer. Gummed paper should be applied to the back of the veneer to stop it splitting. The different pieces should be cut too large rather than too small. Another method, if the old marquetry has been taken off more or less intact, is to use the original as a model, pinning it to the new veneer with veneer pins, with a sheet of plywood as the bottom part of the sandwich, and then cutting.

In marquetry it will be seen that sometimes parts of the veneer, such as the joins of a fan or the contours of a shell, are shaded. This was originally done using heat, and the process can be repeated when it comes to replacement. Silver or flint-sand is placed in a flat tin, and then heated and kept on a hot-plate. The wood to be treated is held in the sand with tweezers. When large areas need to be heat-treated, the sand is deposited directly onto the wood. Where lines need to be drawn, to represent the veins of leaves etc., these can be produced using a hot metal knitting needle or darning needle. These shading techniques will be new to most and it is always a good idea to practise on some old discarded veneer before trying it out on new valued veneer.

In all cases involving replacement of veneer there will be times when the glue oozes out, and this should be mopped up with a moistened cloth. Newly applied veneer can be covered with oiled or waxed paper as additional protection. Sometimes reusable veneer can be removed, though there is a good chance that it will be buckled when it is first taken off, in which case dampen it and press between two warm blocks of wood, making certain that there are no vestiges of glue, then leave to dry. There may be fragments of picture marquetry in rare woods, which can be used in another context. In the eighteenth and nineteenth centuries there was a range of subjects, and it may be that a non-anachronistic flower motif can replace an urn motif, if there is sufficient skill to carry out the project.

Sometimes it may be that stringing or banding needs to be repaired or replaced. Stringing can be removed using a sharp spike, with a hot damp rag to help remove the old glue. Stringing can be bought, but it can also be made, using a steel rule clamped down on the kind of wood you wish to use. The new stringing is then ironed in, using a domestic iron. Brass stringing can also be replaced by poking out the old and ironing in the new.

The same principle applies to the homemade production of banding. Make a sandwich of the woods, and cut off lengths. It is worth mentioning that the central section of banding is often cross-section, and this makes slicing such a length considerably more difficult.

Rather more of a problem is set when veneer needs to be applied to curved surfaces. It is not the removal of old veneer which is difficult, nor the provision of the new veneer, but holding the new veneer in place while the glue is setting. One method is to bend a sheet of hardboard to fit the curved surface, and keep it in place using several cramps. For such jobs, a judiciously placed sandbag can be a great help, as it takes the shape of the object and applies considerable pressure.

When cutting veneer it is often advisable to gum paper to the reverse to prevent splitting, and some restorers prefer to use a sharp knife *with* the grain, but a fine fretsaw *against* the grain. It is always preferable to use veneer that is too thick rather than too thin, as the surface can always be planed down. Sometimes in carcase furniture the wood will twist and turn, causing a fracture in the veneer, in which case a sliver of veneer can be inserted, though it may be preferable to fill in the gap with wax. A simple wax can be made by buying a box of children's wax crayons, selecting likely colours, and melting a few fragments in a tablespoon over heat. As wax is vulnerable to scratching, a thin coat of shellac will offer protection.

There are many stains on the market to help blend in the newly laid veneer. Some are eccentric – a mahogany look can be obtained by mixing an equal quantity of stale beer and water and adding 1tbsp (115ml) of powdered sienna for each pint of the mixture. A walnut stain coupled with a reddish polish will also imitate mahogany. Strong coffee, strained, with powdered Vandyke brown added, is said to give a walnut finish. Some of these stains have a water base, some an oil base, some use methylated spirits, and, considering the variety of colours available, anyone at all skilled in colour matching will be able to key in new veneers. The veneer should be soaked in the stain before application so that the colour penetrates the texture of the wood and is not removed by sanding. The stain is always darker when first applied so the veneer should be allowed to dry out.

XXVII

Woodworm

Attacks of woodworm, the larva of the furniture beetle, should be regarded as somewhat inevitable. Many a choice piece of furniture has been turned down because of the presence of woodworm holes, which may have been there for many years, their occupants long departed. If woodworm holes are seen, the first thing to do is to examine them closely and decide whether they are old or new. Recently made holes have sharp edges, and the inside is clean and bright with a yellowish look. Old woodworm holes will have vestiges of polish and grime. The piece of furniture, if reasonably portable, should be placed at an angle and vigorously tapped. If no wood dust comes out it is likely that any holes are old ones; likely, but not certain, for someone else might have had the same idea and the dust has been scattered.

Ugly as the holes may appear, this is nothing compared with what might have happened in the interior, which may be honeycombed with tiny tunnels, so much so that a sharp blow to an arm or leg of a chair may cause the member to disintegrate. But even furniture far gone may be rescued.

The life-cycle of the furniture beetle is drab and unadventurous. Eggs are laid in crevices and joints on the outside of the furniture, and in due course the eggs hatch and the grubs burrow into the wood, where they remain up to a couple of years before burrowing out again, emerging as fully fledged winged creatures, ready and willing to start laying eggs. The holes are flight-holes. Insecticide such as Rentokil injected into the holes and rubbed on the surfaces and into crevices will hopefully kill any grubs that are on the way in or beetles that are on the way out, though some of the grubs may have penetrated deep into the wood and may be difficult to reach. Furniture nearby should also be treated as the beetle may land elsewhere. Some insecticides are in aerosol form, making general application simple.

The most effective form of treatment is fumigation, but this is hazardous for amateurs and should be left to the experts.

If an attack is severe, and it is feared that the structure of the wood is badly damaged, the part of the furniture in question can be immersed in glue size for several hours, or a thin solution of resin glue can be used. If such an operation is not possible, because the furniture is too unwieldy or the structure of the piece makes it difficult, it is worth considering dismantling the article and immersing the various elements that are at risk. But even such treatment may not be enough if the member – such as a chair leg – is subject to stress and wear and tear, and it may be necessary to replace or let in a strengthening section of wood, which, if it is an antique piece, will greatly reduce the value. If a chair rail or stretcher is contaminated it may be possible to strain them out and release the holding tenons without a demolition job being necessary.

Some woods are more subject to infestation than others. Softwoods are very vulnerable, and walnut is often attacked. Mahogany and oak are usually woodworm free, though where the carcase of the furniture is softwood the woodworm will eat through this and possibly through a mahogany veneer. A simple and trusted method of diverting woodworm away from likely furniture is to provide them with a piece of ash wood. This they adore, and will happily chew their way through this decoy and leave

A made-up cabinet-and-stand c1690. Many original stands collapsed because of the weight of the cabinet or chest. Such pieces, being of walnut, are vulnerable to woodworm.

A seventeenth-century oak dole cupboard. Such pieces are often faked. One device of a faker is to add woodworm holes in excess. Oak is quite resistant to woodworm.

the treasured items alone. Many fakers, unaware of woodworm preferences, provide woodworm holes in their 'old oak', not realising that this does not lend it authenticity.

There is no question that insecticide does do the job it sets out to do. Turpentine and paraffin have a temporary effect, but when they have dried out there is no guarantee that their use is permanent. There is also no question that far too many people are frightened off by the assumed presence of woodworm. Injecting each hole with insecticide can take more time than at first seems likely, and it must be asked if all this effort is worthwhile. For very commonplace furniture it is not. Sometimes there is a border-line case, as, for example, odd stick-back chairs which have been used mainly in kitchens and have therefore been neglected, and incursions by the woodworm ignored or overlooked. As even these workaday chairs are now in some demand, they probably merit treatment. The unseen parts of carcase furniture should always be examined. Often these are not stained or painted, and may be of a softer wood than the rest of the piece.

Once the holes have been treated there arises the need to camouflage the surface. Beeswax mixed with a little shoe polish is one of the favourite methods, rubbed well in so that it penetrates, perhaps poked in when the tunnels are unusually large. An overall waxing will then blend in the treatment material with the general finish.

It is often overlooked that floorboards are sometimes attacked by woodworm, and where it is possible – as for example when moving into a new house – it is advisable to examine them. Nooks and crevices in existing furniture are favourite starting-out points for the furniture beetle, but there is no point in becoming obsessive about it, for the woodworm is an unwelcome visitor which is here to stay and the most one can do is either to furnish solely with oak or mahogany or attempt to curb its inroads.

XXVIII

Refurbishing

Before any refurbishing takes place it is important to make certain that the surfaces are good enough for waxing, polishing, or varnishing. It may be supposed that surface blemishes will disappear when any treatment has been carried out, but although this may sometimes be the case it is not at all certain. Although chairs will get scarred, most superficial damage will occur on the tops of tables, bureaux, chests of drawers, in fact anywhere where a cigarette can be placed, a tea-cup can be laid down, or ink spilled (though with the advent of the ball-point pen this is not much of a contemporary problem and most ink-stains will have almost an antique quality).

Burn marks can be taken out with fine steel wool, a razor blade, a scalpel or craft knife, and it is important to get rid of any charring. The resulting shallow hole can be filled in a number of ways. Artists' oil-colours can work very well, worked in with the finger tips. Mixed with linseed oil, a made-up medium, or a varnish the oil-paint will be glossy; mixed with turpentine it will be matt. The choice depends on whether the entire surface is to be polished. A filler can also be made from coloured beeswax, from powder stain mixed with a medium such as epoxy resin, or shellac mixed with powder pigment. The traditional filler is known as beaumontage, made by mixing equal quantities of beeswax and rosin, with a few flakes of shellac added. This mixture is melted in a tin, and powdered colour is added, burnt umber for dark oak, and red ochre for mahogany, but a number of tints are available and almost any match can be made.

Heat marks take the form of white circular patches, and equal quantities of turpentine and linseed oil should be mixed and applied with a soft warm cloth, using a good deal of elbow grease. This mixture should be allowed to penetrate, and then a rag impregnated with vinegar should be used, rubbing with the grain. An alternative method is to use methylated spirits applied sparingly to a pad, and rubbed over with a quick smooth action. Cigar ash mixed with water makes a mild abrasive and can also be used to get rid of heat marks.

Black spots and rings can be confused with burns, but actually they are discolourations due to prolonged contact with water. A solution of oxalic acid crystals is advised, brushed over the mark, and wiped off. An old toothbrush is ideal as an applicator. 3 heaped tbsp (405ml) in a cup of hot water will be ample, though some restorers prefer a milder solution. Although oxalic acid will not harm furniture, it is poisonous and care must be taken when using it.

The same method can be used to remove ink stains, or domestic bleach used undiluted may well provide the answer. If the mark disappears the bleach should be washed off with water. Nitric acid, used in a weak solution, is more potent, but can leave its own marks, which can be treated with linseed oil. The question must be asked whether ink stains should be removed at all, for they often appear on high-value pieces of furniture such as desks and bureaux and sometimes the stains have mellowed so much that they are acceptable.

The same applies to scratches. All antique furniture is bound to have its quota of scratches, and many collectors prefer to have their furniture in a used state rather than try to bring it up to showroom condition. If scratches do not penetrate below the polish level they can be taken out by fine glasspaper dipped into linseed oil, though this may necessitate repolishing. Deeper scratches can be filled with coloured wax, rubbed across the scratch, and levelled with fine glasspaper. Filler can always be applied by brush. Small scratches which show up white can often be treated by rubbing the exposed face of a broken brazil nut kernel across them. Newly made scratches may seem to demand immediate treatment, as the scar may seem utterly unacceptable, but with a waxing or a polishing they may well turn out to be inoffensive. Scratches which are beginning to merge into cracks, not serious enough to merit the insertion of slivers of wood, can be filled with beeswax, pressed in with a hot metal rod such as a knitting or darning needle, or perhaps an electric soldering iron.

Highly polished furniture is sometimes marred by the presence of tiny hair lines or cracks, caused by lack of oil in the varnish used in the finish, and an old remedy for this was to mix 1 part of lemon oil with 2 parts of boiled linseed oil, and apply at regular intervals. Finger marks and foggy patches show on furniture where too much polish has been used, and these can be removed by wiping the surface with an up and down movement, using a soft cloth moistened in warm water and then wrung very dry. The surface should be dried immediately, and then rubbed with an oiled cloth. Grease spots can be removed from polished surfaces using soapy water, wiped dry, and then rubbed with a solution of alcohol and turpentine. An old method of removing obstinate grease stains is to make a paste of powdered soap and ammonia, apply for two days, and then wash off.

The process of filling small holes and cracks is known as stopping, and although wax is a basic method another involves the use of shellac. A small quantity of shellac flakes is melted in a shallow tin on a hotplate, but on no account must it be allowed to bubble. When it is liquid mix in dry pigments, stirring well, then tilt tin, scraping the mixture together at the same time as the tin is removed from the heat. As the mixture cools a ball of this stopping is twisted on the end of a stick, which is then rolled on paper to make a cylinder. If the stopping solidifies, reheat. The stopping is inserted in a malleable state, as with beeswax, and any excess is removed with a sharp chisel before glasspaper or silicone carbide paper is used to perfect the surface. Rather than bother to do this, a restorer can buy stick stopping, which looks like sealing-wax, and is applied under heat as with the beeswax method outlined above.

The decision whether to wax, polish or varnish is not one to be taken lightly. It is now more than a hundred and seventy years since French polishing was introduced to this country, and for a time anything that stood still was subject to this treatment, including the most unsuitable. Marquetry was stripped down, and fine lacquer was obliterated. The results of haphazard French polishing can sometimes be seen in white flecks in the grain of furniture surfaces. These are vestiges of plaster of paris used to fill the grain without the wood having been properly sealed, or the results of the original filler being used without colouring. To remove these flecks it is necessary to get rid of any existing polish and rub down with glasspaper and linseed oil.

It is a matter of some conjecture how antique furniture was originally treated, but certainly from very early times it was realised that without some kind of finish valued furniture would suffer damage. Sealing the grain could be accomplished in many ways, and perhaps the customary way was to varnish and then wax. It must also be remembered that much furniture was painted, and the colour was applied on the wax.

Some painted furniture has over the years been restored to the condition it was in

Basic no-nonsense furniture such as this George II mahogany chest of about 1750 is best left alone, merely cleaned and waxed.

before the paint was put on, but, especially in pine, present-day dealers realise that colour can be a selling point, and pine furniture that has ruthlessly been stripped with caustic soda is being painted, then part stripped, so that it might seem that the painting is contemporary with the piece. Often these restorers overplay their hand, and attempt to paint flowers and motifs, very characteristic of Bavarian pine. In most cases this artistry is incompetent and anachronistic and fails to enhance the furniture in any way.

Traces of paint in holes and the hidden facets of carving or decoration do not necessarily mean that this is original work. Throughout the years items of furniture which seemed to the owners to be a little dull have been renovated, and in the past furniture which today can be worth several thousand pounds was regarded as of little consequence, perhaps given a coat of paint and put in the nursery or passed on to servants or retainers, who had no hesitation in cannibalising it, converting it, or decorating it to their own tastes. So we have furniture oddities which confuse the sale-rooms, and clocks which have been cut down to fit into low-ceilinged cottages.

Oak was varnished and waxed, and walnut was probably given several coats of varnish, each being rubbed down when dry, and then waxed. Sheraton states that in his day mahogany was treated with linseed oil, and finished with a mixture of linseed oil and brickdust. The diverse colouring of eighteenth-century mahogany, from honey to deep red, may not only depend on the source of the mahogany but on its initial treatment.

When a piece of furniture is bought, and the condition is all but acceptable, it may be sufficient to apply what is known as a 'reviver.' There are various recipes to concoct a reviver. Vinegar and water is the simplest. Another recipe is raw linseed oil with white spirit, in equal proportions, with a dash of vinegar, known as 'half-and-half' in the trade. Or raw linseed oil, methylated spirits, and vinegar in equal parts. A more complicated mixture can be made up of 1 cupful of vinegar, 1 cupful of methylated spirits, 1oz (30g) of camphor, 1oz (25ml) of raw linseed oil, and ½oz (15g) of butter of antimony.

It is very much a matter of opinion. Soap and water can work wonders, wiping dry as soon as possible and not letting the water settle. Many professionals use a weak solution of household soda, but if this mixture is too strong it will begin to affect existing polish or varnish. Household soda is also used to darken oak and mahogany.

If the condition is too far gone for cleaning or reviving, and the piece of furniture has previously been French polished, this finish can be lifted by using a lint-free rag and methylated spirits, used evenly over the surface (methylated spirits is one of the constituents of French polish). If there is dirt and grime, use fine steel wool with methylated spirits, not rubbing too hard, and dry steel wool will get rid of the white streaks resulting from old plaster of paris residue in the grain.

With the provision of excellent ready-made French polishes much of the mystique has gone out of this arcane process, but with valuable pieces of furniture it might well be asked if it is best left to a professional restorer. Though it must be remembered that it is all reversable, that the hours of work can be cancelled out.

The basic principles of French polishing are, (remembering that patience is of the essence), to prepare the surface, sanding if necessary, stain if required, then brush on two coats of French polish. If grain needs filling, rub in plaster of paris tinted with powder colour to match surrounding wood. Pumice is sometimes used, especially on new wood. When the plaster of paris is dry, linseed oil should be applied thinly all over the surface to be treated, and rubbed down with very fine glasspaper. The wood should then be wiped completely dry in preparation for the French polishing.

What French polish to use? Some of these have strange names, such as button polish (this type comes in solid button shapes). White is used for light wood, button is yellowish, orange is a golden brown, garnet a dark brown, and black should be used for ebony or ebonised woods (most likely a close-grained wood such as pear or cherry). Transparent, as the title suggests, gives the natural colour of the wood being polished.

French polish is not applied with a brush but with what is known as a rubber, consisting of a square of wadding folded then wrapped in a square of cloth (old sheeting, handkerchief, linen). The unfolded wadding should measure approximately

10in x 10in (25cm x 25cm), the wrapping the same. Polish should be poured on the wadding a little at a time, squeezed with the thumb until it oozes through the linen. When not being used the rubber should be kept in an air-tight container. There are various methods advised in folding the rubber, but the main thing is to keep the wadding inside rather than having bits trailing outside the linen. The most straightforward method is to draw up the linen on all sides, and twist at the top so that you have a mushroom shaped pad.

The rubber should be used in gentle straight strokes with the grain, from one end to the other. If there is drag, recharge with polish, but on no account should the rubber stick to the surface. Several coats need to be applied, with drying time between. Towards the end of the process, which can be quite lengthy, linseed oil should be added. This lubricates the surface; and it prevents the rubber lifting the polish already laid down. As little oil should be used as possible, just a smear. The degree of 'pull' can only be learned from experience; some say that it should feel like pulling the hand across a pane of glass.

Finally, a new rubber should be prepared with fresh wadding and a fresh outer cloth, and this passed over the surface in a circular motion, then a figure of eight action, finishing with backwards and forwards strokes with the grain. A touch of linseed oil should be applied to the rubber, and later, six hours or so, removed with a soft cloth dampened with methylated spirits. This is called 'spiriting off'. An alternative process does not use methylated spirits. The ordinary rubber, or one specially made, is used almost dry, with very little polish. The aim is to lift the oil left in the earlier state. The linseed oil is simply not wanted any more. For carvings and ornamental pieces French polish should be applied with a sable brush, thinned with 25 per cent of methylated spirits.

How is it possible to tell whether a surface has been previously French polished? Put a drop of methylated spirits on an unimportant corner and see if the surface blisters and dissolves. If it does, it is French polish. French polishing should be done in warm surroundings – not less than 18°C (65°F), and humidity should be low. Low temperatures and dampness in the air cause the polish to 'bloom', to exude a whiteness.

Functional and disastrous to good furniture, polyurethane lacquer is resistant to heat as French polishing is not, and acceptable for useful or brand-new furniture of little account. It is good on pine, because it hardens it. It should be diluted with white spirit or turpentine when first applied on softwoods, so that it soaks in. For the best results, several coats should be applied, rubbed down with glasspaper in between applications. Beeswax applied on steel wool will give a pleasant gloss to pine.

Colouring or staining wood can be carried out using water-based, spirit-based, oil, or chemical methods. After fixing the surface with two wipes of a shellac (French polishing) rubber, water staining should be carried out using thin coats, with shellac fixing between. The standard stain for oak is Vandyke, originally a coloured pigment from walnut husks, bought in crystal and powder form. When the powder is used, it should be added to hot water in a large flat tin a teaspoon at a time, kept stirred, and when forming a thick paste, smoothed with a palette knife and allowed to cool. When needed for use, water is added so that the consistency is of thin cream. It should be applied with a brush but distributed with a rubber. It has to be done rapidly for the water evaporates. Vandyke is slightly abrasive, and should not be rubbed too hard. A

thick mix should be used with ornament or carvings, and the highlights wiped off immediately.

Bichromate of potash crystals are useful for staining mahogany. Diluted well, the result is a reddish brown, while a stronger solution gives a medium brown. The user has to wait until the wood is dry before he knows exactly what colour he has got. Domestic bleach will reverse staining which has got out of hand. Bichromate of potash is poisonous and should be used wearing rubber gloves; if this is not done the user's hands will be stained orange, probably not irreversably. Oil staining takes longer to dry and one has less control over the process. Spirit staining, using methylated spirits, can be reversed by using the shellac rubber.

With such a variety of stains commercially available most colours can be obtained, using the methods outlined above. For those who wish to do so, graining can be faked by mixing French polish with powdered black pigment and applied with a feather, or by mixing ½oz (15g) of sulphate of iron in 1pt (560ml) of water, also applied with a feather.

No harm can be done by simple waxing. First of all the piece of furniture is washed with soap and water, a small area at a time, without the water being allowed to settle. Then wiped thoroughly dry. There are many excellent proprietary brands of wax such as *Antiquax* but many restorers prefer to make their own, finding that ready-made wax is too soft. Many add carnauba wax, a hard wax from Brazil, to the mix. A traditional recipe is:

> Carnauba wax 2 parts (by volume)
> Paraffin wax 2 parts
> Beeswax 1 part
> Pure turpentine 10 parts

Another recipe:

> Carnauba wax 2 parts
> Beeswax 12 parts
> Turpentine 120 parts

A 1925 recipe for a wax proposes the use of ordinary floor wax, to which is added a little linseed oil, stain, and turpentine, melted together and applied with a brush while still in liquid form.

So it will be seen that there is no definitive version. Beeswax should be the unrefined brown not the refined white. If a dark wax is wanted brown or black shoe polish should be added. When melting waxes place them in a large tin, no more than a third full to allow for stirring. The wax should be heated, but not to the point where it is smoking. There is an advisable order – carnauba wax, paraffin wax, beeswax, then any colouring agent, with turpentine last of all as the wax melts. The turpentine should be added gently, a spoonful at a time. Make certain that the wax is off the heat as otherwise the whole lot can go up in flames. After a good stirring, the result should be a butter-like substance.

The wax should be applied in small areas with a circular motion, and any excess should be removed with a clean dry rag. Do not try for an immediate shine. This comes with a buffing with muttoncloth or corduroy. A good wax finish should last for six

A flashy piece such as this Regency sofa table (above) can take a high finish; a Chippendale-style chair (below) cannot.

months. There may be a temporary bloom, but this will soon go. Wax should be applied to carvings and mouldings with a brush. Wax can be used over other finishes, but other finishes should not be used over wax. Turpentine or white spirit reverses any waxing, used with steel wool with the grain, cleaned off with a turpentine-impregnated cloth, and wiped dry.

Linseed oil used by itself can also make a good finish on hardwoods, and should be rubbed on strenuously at regular intervals. One sixty-year-old method of oiling advises the use of a piece of old carpet weighted by a brick as a polisher. As with old wax, a surface treated with linseed oil can be reversed by the use of turpentine.

Varnishes come in two varieties, oil and spirit. One disadvantage of oil varnish is that dust tends to gather during the somewhat lengthy drying-off time. A rather soft brush should be used so that the bristles will not make their own surface texture, and the action should be up-and-down and backwards-and-forwards, never circular. The number of coats depends on taste, but earlier coats should be diluted with turpentine or white spirit. An average treatment consists of three coats. Between coats, the surface should be rubbed down with linseed oil on a rag with perhaps a little pumice powder added, making certain that the pumice is not evident when the time comes to apply the next coat.

Spirit varnish dries rapidly, and the surface of the wood should be sealed with two brush strokes of French polish before starting. A very soft brush should be used, only with the grain of the wood, and between coats fine steel wool should be used to rub down.

Over-use of varnish in the past has much to answer for, and the Victorians applied coat after coat in reckless abandon until the texture and the character of the wood had completely disappeared. As they did the same thing to their oil paintings it seems to have been a natural failing. Fortunately the varnish they used is easily removable.

It may be possible to remove old unwanted finishes with the minimum of effort, but there may come a time when the need is for stripping. This operation is mainly associated with pine, and a medley of consequent disasters following immersion in the stripping tank – uneven, washed-out colouring; loose joints, occasional disintegration. A thin non-caustic solvent-wash is advised, perhaps trisodium phospate (TSP). This is used freely in quantity, and quickly, being poured on if necessary and kept on the move. It is wiped off with a rag, and the surface is rubbed gently with fine steel wool. Methylated spirits or warm water with distilled vinegar is then applied, and then the wood is cleaned with a dry rag. Sometimes it may be necessary to use a scraper on ingrained paint. Stains on bare timber can be countered with oxalic acid. In some old furniture, a milk-based paint was used, and this can be taken off with ammonia, used outside and with rubber gloves, and applied with steel wool. Rinse with warm water. Many strippers raise the grain, and if this happens rub down with steel wool.

Ammonia is a very useful if dangerous agent. It is used to darken oak, either using a brush – when its darkening capacity can be halted by the application of domestic bleach – or by placing the piece of furniture in an enclosed cupboard or space and letting the ammonia fumes do their work. This process is known as fuming, and was widely used by the Victorians who liked their oak to have the true Elizabethan look, or what they thought was the true Elizabethan look.

For heavy stripping, add ¼lb (110g) of caustic soda to 2pt (1.12 litres) of water in a bucket. Never the other way around as it spits. It is advisable to wear protective

156

clothing though many professionals never bother and their hands and arms are covered with what might appear to be freckles but are actually burn marks from the caustic. Use with a mop, and when the paint or finish has dissolved, which it will do sometimes with great rapidity, sluice down, wipe dry, and swab down with a vinegar solution. For stubborn paint use a stiff brush, a knife, and a scraper. Do not subject good furniture to this treatment. And stripping with caustic soda works better when the weather is warm. If working in a garden, it is worth remembering that caustic soda is not the best thing for grass, shrubs or plants.

The ultimate in furniture harassment is bleaching. A mild version is involved in removing stains which have been applied to the wood, and household bleach is used, in various strengths depending on how it is going. It is wise to test on an unseen part of the furniture. The bleach should be rinsed off with water, and left to dry to ascertain whether the task has been accomplished. Bleach which takes out the colour of the wood and transforms it into something else comes in a two-part pack. This is fairly potent, and goggles and rubber gloves should be worn. Some restorers ignore the instructions and have their own individual methods, but novices should be wary of following their example. Vinegar stops the action of the bleach.

Although bleaching should be used with discretion, and never on antique furniture, if there is any furniture which needs looking at afresh with a view to turning it into something else, bleaching it in a sense wipes the slate clean: it gives the adventurous a spur, ridding the piece of its old connections and turning it into raw material ripe for exploitation.

Refurbishment means not only bringing old furniture up to concert pitch; it means bringing it up, and then gently throwing it out of tune again. Many people who own antique furniture wish it to be known that it is exactly that, and not a clever reproduction. The way to do this is to introduce signs of wear and tear. Too much energy will result in scratches, maybe the odd broken moulding, maybe the smashing of the occasional carving. So there has to be a middle way. If it seems incomprehensible to deliberately damage a valuable piece of furniture, then you belong to a sterling body of opinion, but it is done, and it will continue to be done.

There are several methods, such as placing gravel pebbles in a plastic bag and swinging it at the furniture so that the results are picturesque, and no doubt convincing, dents which are shaded in with Vandyke tint. Others prefer to whack the furniture with chains, or a padded mallet. And it is not altogether unknown for fake antique oak furniture to be distressed by leaving it outside to face the ravages of the weather for a few months.

XXIX

Transformation

Transformation of ordinary furniture into something a little bit special is not a new idea, and in the 1920s it was a major do-it-yourself activity. Some of the ideas may strike us as horrendous; but others were in keeping with modern ideas of revitalising furniture. The preparation was not so different from that used today, bearing in mind

In the 1930s such furniture as this Charles I oak press cupboard of the 1650s was treated in a very cavalier fashion, often remodelled to conform to contemporary taste.

that sixty years ago there was not the wealth of products available. A quotation from an article in the magazine *Ideal Home* will demonstrate this:

> The furniture was originally of a very ordinary kind, painted cream and with little but its practical utility to recommend it. The wood was first very carefully washed with strong soda water and then rubbed down with fine sandpaper to remove any unevenness. Had the furniture been made of wood of a very coarse grain it would have been wise to coat it first with filling. This is prepared by making a paste of whitening and water and adding a little plaster of Paris and powdered glue. The mixture must be kept warm in a jar standing in hot water and be applied very thinly. When it is dry the wood is again rubbed down with fine sandpaper.

Sometimes it was desired to turn the piece into dark furniture by the application of ebony stain which 'imparted to wardrobe, bed and chairs a rich glossy appearance closely resembling lacquer . . . for the dressing table real Chinese lacquer was used'. Both the black and red 'lacquer' were decorated with gold, as 'inspiration was gained by a visit to a museum exhibiting Chinese lacquer furniture'.

The design was first lightly traced in pencil and then picked out in gold with a fine brush. The gold was made by using a gold bronze powder in a bronze medium, or by using gold size. This could be dulled down to give an antique effect by dusting over when nearly dry with gold powder.

This treatment could be effective, or it could be ludicrous, as when applied to a standard cast-iron fireplace, or when a contemporary wardrobe was decked out with meaningless Chinese patterns above the central mirrored door. On the other hand, the panels of a door picked out with gold against black come off well. As with all transformation work, much depends on the taste of the person doing the work, and for those without skill but who still wished to pep up their furniture there were transfers, cut-outs for sticking on suitable furniture, or stencils, produced in large numbers for what seems to have been a booming market. Occasionally some of these homely conversions turn up, in household auctions or second-hand shops, but time has not been kind to them. The colours are fading, and where transfers have been applied these are almost transparent, representing the ghost of the original.

Much of the furniture made in the 1920s, when design had lost its way, was mediocre, and no-one can blame its owners from being bored with it and wishing to give it a certain individuality. Some of the treatments are very original, and have not been revived. For example, what can be done with mirrors? Do you fancy scraping off

A lacquered 'Chinese' cabinet of the 1920s. Transforming mundane pieces of furniture into something more interesting is not new; DIY enthusiasts of the 1920s lacquered anything which moved!

159

some of the silvered back with a sharp blade and painting a little picture, using a medium equal parts of amber varnish, copal varnish, and linseed oil? The result could be incredibly awful. But worth considering is backing a mirror not with silver but with black or colours.

There is sufficient reflection for most purposes, and the effect in a room of dark papers and furniture is striking enough to make the experiment worthwhile. All one has to do is to lay a sheet of glass absolutely flat on a table, preferably newspaper-covered. Flatness can be assured by the simple test of laying an ordinary marble on its surface; if the marble rolls, the glass obviously needs adjustment, though a spirit level can also be used and is just as accurate. One then spills a pool of common black varnish all over the surface. Red, dark blue, in fact any colour that is opaque, can be applied in exactly the same way and, set in an antique frame, such a mirror has at least the charm of rarity.

The question dying to be asked is how many valuable antique mirrors were subject to this treatment? And that is the danger of enthusiastically espousing the cause of transformation. In the past, valuable pieces of furniture have been carved up, cut down, cannibalised to make something else. And there is no guarantee that this will not happen time and time again. Of course, it happens with objects other than furniture; the lids of eighteenth-century enamel boxes (now worth several hundred pounds) were taken off to provide pictures for dolls' houses. Pieces of Elizabethan silver were given spouts by unscrupulous silversmiths and transformed into teapots because teapots were in demand, and it did not matter much that Queen Elizabeth and her contemporaries knew nothing of tea.

And so we come to modern transformations. One of the aims is to make wood appear to be something else. This is not new. The Victorians made wooden pillars and marbled them so successfully that only when they were moved was it apparent that they were not quite what they looked. During the Regency period other woods were used to simulate bamboo, reproducing the joints and the markings with great skill.

When we are dealing with good furniture there is a reluctance to be too cavalier. Modern methods are scorned by furniture restorers as they will denigrate the furniture and are often processes that cannot be reversed. But when transforming something of no quality, anything goes, and they can be used with gusto. The furniture to be used goes under a number of names; boarding-house furniture, office furniture, thirties repro, shipping goods. Some of it will be of softwood, some of oak, and the backs of carcase furniture may be of plywood, which doesn't matter. Often the fronts of 1930s furniture will be five-ply plywood with a veneer.

The first thing to do, after buying it – and buying it with transformation in mind – is to look at the condition. There may be no need to strip it down. If the paint is worn and patchy it can be painted over; if the paint is holding up well, it can still be painted over, or the original colour can be incorporated in the final effect (by partially taking off a top coat and revealing part of the underlying basic colour). Otherwise, for smaller items a proprietary paint stripper such as Nitromors can be used. Metal fitments can be taken off, drawers withdrawn, and doors taken off. Caustic soda can be used for large pieces. Sandpaper or steel wool can be used to clean up, but as there is no need for timidity an electric sander can come in handy.

There is a choice of primers. One of the standards is white oil-based, used 3 parts primer, 1 part white spirit or turpentine, applied thickly and brushed well in.

Lloyd Loom furniture is often subject to transformation as it is still about in quantity and is still cheap.

The kind of uninspired 1880s furniture of little value which can be profitably transformed.

A curious piece of furniture, actually a German bureau about 1730. As it does not fit into the accepted canons of eighteenth-century furniture, the owner may well consider its potential for transformation.

Aluminium primer is good for varnished surfaces, and saves the time of stripping. Acrylic primer is one of the successes of modern technology; it covers well, dries quickly, and can be painted on almost immediately.

Unknown to traditional restorers is knot sealer, used especially on softwoods before priming as knots exude sap for a considerable time, which can break through a paint covering. To fill the grain proprietary fillers are used, mixed to a cream, and applied with and then against the grain. The filled and primed surface should be sanded down; then there is an option of two coats of shellac, giving a silk-sheen surface. It may not be necessary. Undercoat can be applied in one or two coats, then sanded down. A modern replacement for the three-stage filler, primer, undercoat operation is synthetic gesso, more expensive than traditional gesso (plaster and glue size), applied in several coats with sanding down between each. The choice of abrasive is up to the user: glasspaper, steel wool, silicon carbide (wet-and-dry), all have their adherents.

So is the choice of paints up to the user. Water-based such as emulsion, oil-based, and acrylic can all be used, and all varnished over. The main emphasis is on more than one coat of the base colour, giving the bottom layer time to thoroughly dry. A semi-transparent paint can be made by mixing oil colour with polyurethane clear varnish. Gloss can be removed by going over with steel wool. Where there is to be a design on a base layer, two coats of shellac or a coat of polyurethane varnish will make a suitable sealer and provide a good working surface.

Transformation may just mean painting the furniture flatly with unusual colours or colour combinations, picking out the design features in different colours or lining or striping in a contrasting colour. Professionals can draw or paint a straight line freehand; amateurs, by and large, cannot. So a straight-edge needs to be used, with a pencil or felt-tip pen to mark out the lining to be done. Sometimes the ordinary straight-edge, a 12in (30cm) ruler, will not be long enough, and folding rules are not altogether satisfactory as when a pencil line is done with one there is often a tiny bump where the rule is hinged. It is better to use a piece of batten about a metre in length, preferably chamfered.

There are two valuable short cuts to lining. One is to use masking tape to mark out the side of the line (or two pieces of masking tape to mark out both sides, so that you just paint the area exposed). Acrylic tape is best for this. The second tip is to draw in the line or stripe in pencil, (both sides of the line – even if the line is only ¼in (5mm) wide), then take a craft knife or a scalpel and gently trace over it. When the paint is applied, freehand, without the need to use tape, you will find that the channel

Transformation is not a modern fad, as can be seen from this 1926 advertisement. The nursery furniture is ordinary trade furniture painted white.

made by the knife will stop the paint spreading over onto the area you want to keep plain.

You don't have to use straight lines. You can use curves and arcs, easier to do than straight lines. If you wish to incorporate circles in your design you fix a small sable paint brush in the socket side of a pair of compasses instead of a pencil. This gives an immediate effect, without the need to go over pencil lines with a brush. Templates made from transparent plastic called French curves and available from drawing-office equipment retailers are invaluable in providing a wide range of shapes.

Lining edges is much simpler than interior lining because there is only one side to be considered. But if there is a tendency to wobble as you paint the lining in, recourse can always be had to masking tape. Masking tape is sufficiently adhesive to hold fast as it is being used, but unlike other adhesive tapes it is removed easily without hurting the underlying layer of paint. And it tears easily with the fingers, so that there is not the nuisance of searching for a pair of scissors to cut off lengths.

Do not trust your eye when measuring distances. If, for example, you are going to line a table-top, with a border inset 4in (10cm) all round, measure it. Then, when you have put in the line in pencil (or felt-tip – it rubs off better), measure it again before applying the paint. If a mistake has been made, try not to codge it up, but take off all the top detail, leaving the undercoat, and start again. That is why it is often a good idea to seal the undercoat. If there is a chance of error, and you are using water-based paint, it is better to use gouache or water-colour rather than acrylic, as it sponges off immediately.

The range of colours available in all kinds of media is incredible, and of course there is gold, silver and aluminium in the form of metal powders, used on a tacky varnished or shellac surface, and applied with a piece of chamois leather or velvet on the finger, either directly or using a stencil. These metal powders are inclined to blow away easily, so make certain there is no draught. Metal leaf is available in booklet form mounted on tissue. Size is painted onto the area to be covered, left until it is slightly tacky, and the metal leaf is pressed down, tissue-side up, any loose bits brushed off with a sable brush after first removing the tissue. If a fairly large area needs to be covered, the metal leaf is used overlapping. It may not be necessary to go to these lengths. A cheaper substitute for gold and silver is gold and silver poster paint, bought in small jars, which has very good covering ability.

A distinct kind of finish can be got by sponging, using thinned-down paint in different colours or shades of the one colour, applied with a sponge (preferably a natural one and not a household imitation, unless this provides just the texture you want). Before sponging, and if using an oil-based paint, the surface should be slightly filmy, so that the colour rides, not making just a blotch. Such a surface can be provided by a solution of five parts turpentine or white spirit to one of linseed oil, applied thinly.

The sponged colours can be built up gradually, or applied in full colour from the start. Hard edges may not be wanted, and these can be blended away with a soft brush. Water-based paints can be applied directly onto gesso, which absorbs water and leaves a faded image, and also on emulsion before it is quite dry. Acrylic lends itself to endless variations; diluted, it is a slightly grainy watercolour that dries rapidly, and will blend with emulsion to give a very subtle effect.

Spattering is an equally simple operation, and can be used on a dry or wet surface,

Every picture tells a story. Is this a desirable acquisition? Is it some exquisite piece of Victorian Gothic? No, it is an early telegraphic machine.

Left: Mass-produced tea-trolley of ambiguous date, of little value but surprisingly useful, both for its original purpose and for hard usage in greenhouse, workshop, or playroom, as it is all but indestructible. *Right:* An Art Deco dressing table given the full transformation treatment.

An Edwardian display cabinet in its setting. It is important to visualise items of furniture as a part of living, not as collectables merely appreciating in value.

166

James I court cupboard of about 1610 in good unaltered condition and selling for £4,620.

where the tiny flecks of paint will turn into stains. It is better to do spattering on wet with the surface horizontal, for otherwise the paint will run down. As with sponging, colours can be distinct or shades of one colour, or oil- or water-based. Any old brush will do if the bristles are stiff; a brush past its prime can have its bristles partly cut off. The paint to spatter should be thin, and the brush should be poked gently into it. The spatter will be more controllable with a finger, but a knife blade, a ruler, or a suitable piece of wood can be used. The finger is passed over the bristle tips, and the paint is flicked on. Diluted acrylic is recommended, as it dries rapidly, and the process can be regulated.

Spattering can create amazing effects, imitating natural stone such as porphyry. The bottom terracotta coat of paint is applied with a sponge rather than a brush, to give a slightly uneven texture, and then the surface is spattered with cream, left to dry, then spattered with thin black paint. A very fine spray can be obtained by using an atomizer; the same principle is adopted in the commercial artist's air-brush. But the paint must be thin, otherwise it clogs in next to no time. A thoroughly easy method is to use an empty Windolene spray.

By using templates or stencils a set design can be spattered on a plain surface, and many commercial firms supply a whole range of stencils, which can be used as they come, or you can use parts of one and parts of another. Stencils can be made from card. The design is sketched out in pencil and then cut with a sharp craft knife or a scalpel. Stencils, of course, can be used in the orthodox manner on flat-painted surfaces, and give a much more professional feel than hand-painting. The stencil is held against the surface by hand or by using masking tape, and the paint is applied by brush, quickly and crisply. Acrylic paint is ideal for stencils, as it dries rapidly and when the stencil is taken away the paint won't run.

Another substance that can be imitated is tortoise shell, using an orange background, on which slightly diluted dark varnish is applied, and black oil-paint added with a pointed soft brush, allowed to blend in until the required texture is obtained. The orange base will dimly come through giving a luminous effect. Tortoise shelling is a typical transformation operation; it can be as complex or as simple as the user wants. It can turn out not to be like tortoise shell at all, but a fun finish, never seen before. Malachiting is one of the favourite finishes, a subtle striated dark green, and several antique dealers have gone into this commercially, using quite good quality furniture.

Marbling is one of the most difficult finishes, but if successful it can be staggering. Veins are painted onto a wet glossy oil-based surface using a small sable brush. A jerky jagged motion should be used. The veins are then softened using a dry brush, brushing across them; excess paint is taken off using a tissue or a small fragment of sponge and this residue is relocated elsewhere. The dry brush is used again, across the veining, and when the surface is dry extra veining is added, some in white.

Acrylic can also be used in this process, using a retarder which slows down the drying time. If the surface is really wet, the veining can be dragged through, and the water will soften the edges immediately in a convincing manner. Blotting-paper is used where necessary to remove surplus water or paint, or for getting rid of harsh outlines. For imitating natural substances an acrylic varnish should not be used, as this gives a matt finish. An ordinary polyurethane varnish is preferable. Of course, there are various types of marble that can be emulated, not only the veined white. It is important not to overdo the veining, or to make it too systematic; it should not look like a wobbly mesh. In some marble the veining is very fragmentary, and does not appear to go anywhere. It is traditional to do the veining diagonally, though there is no reason why this should be the case.

This is an area for adventure. Some of the 'new' methods, such as Chinese lacquering using heavily laid-down paint, are ancient; some are absolutely novel. And manufacturers are realising that furniture transformation, along with new ways of looking at interiors and interior fittings, is an expanding market. Mention must be made of the new range of Ronseal coloured varnishes, used singly or in combination.

Treated furniture is for use, splendid for interior decoration and imaginative schemes, but it is very doubtful whether even the best marbled or malachited furniture will appreciate in value. Some day when boarding-house furniture, shipping goods, or chain-store furniture reaches the status of antiques no doubt these finishes will be stripped off to reveal what lies underneath – oak, pine, deal, and plywood!

PART III

APPENDICES

Buying and Selling Furniture

Furniture can be bought from a wide variety of sources, from auction rooms, antiques shops, second-hand shops, junk shops, antiques fairs and markets, street markets, boot sales and privately. If you are spending a good deal of money, and want a guarantee that what you have bought is what it purports to be, a good-quality antiques shop should be first on the list, as the owner, if asked, will give you a detailed description, and if he or she is wrong you have redress. The cataloguer of an auction room will describe an article to be sold, but auctioneers are only human, and can err, and if you read the small print on their catalogues you will find that they absolve themselves from blame if there is an error of description. Nor can they be held responsible for any damage that they don't spot.

When buying at auction, have no fear that the auctioneer is going to put something down to you because you blew your nose or winked at someone. If there is any doubt at all, he will ask you if you are bidding. Once you have bought one item, it will register, and you will have no difficulty in getting his attention if you bid again. Auctioneers are professionals; their aim is to get through about ninety lots an hour without hold-ups. After the sale is finished they still have a lot of work to do.

Almost everyone buys something at auction on impulse. 'That's cheap!' you mutter, and your hand goes up, though the object being pointed out by the porter has not been examined previously. It may be that it *is* cheap. It may be that you may have put in a bid on top of the dealers'-ring spokesman's bid. But it may be that there is something wrong with it, and it has reached its level. It may be a good buy, but out of fashion. At a time when 'brown' furniture was riding high, ebonised furniture of equal quality was being ignored because it was not liked in the trade (though it was actually quite popular with the general public).

If possible, always view a sale the day before, not just before the sale starts. It takes longer to go round a thousand lots than many realise. Mark your catalogue clearly with the lots you are interested in, and the top price you are prepared to pay. Pick an odd number: 52 instead of 50, 160 instead of 150, so that you just pip those who have settled for a round figure.

The top flight of antiques fairs and markets are as good as antiques shops. The stall-holders have a reputation to uphold, and they too will guarantee an article, if asked. And if they know. For a dealer may have a fine piece of furniture, at top price, without knowing much about it except that it has all the appearance of being genuine. In the antiques trade, instinct is often as important as knowledge.

It is up to the buyer to satisfy him- or herself that there are no hidden damages or

Opposite, above: A piece that is always sought after. A breakfront bookcase of about 1815, sold in 1988 for £3,740.
Below: The classic chair which in a long set can have no upper limit value-wise. A set of eight of these George III shield-back chairs in the Hepplewhite mode sold for £13,750 in 1989.

171

A splendid seventeenth-century oak gateleg table, simple, straightforward, combining the useful with the appealing.

faults. Fortunately damage to furniture is much easier to spot than damage to porcelain, if the inspection of an item is methodical. If it is a chair, turn it upside down, examine the joints, look closely to ascertain that there are no major repairs and that pieces of wood have not been let into the structure. Such repairs may be acceptable but they might also be significant – a fillet of wood might be let in because a previous section was wormy. If it is a set of chairs, examine each one, compare one with another. One might have been damaged, and the damaged bits have been spread around to make them less conspicuous. And make certain that they all match. In the old days, crafty antiques dealers sold 'in the dark'. In the gloom at the backs of their shops they kept furniture which was not all it seemed. Sometimes they compromised with a 15-watt bulb.

With 'carcase' furniture such as chests of drawers, take each drawer out, making certain that they all belong, that they run easily, and that the handles or knobs are acceptable, and, if replacements, in keeping. Look behind the front of the drawer for old holes, pieces of wood or dowels put in to fill old holes, where handles of a different type were once fixed. If the back of the chest of drawers is rough, or painted an orangy-brown, this may be authentic, but make a note of it, and ask.

Always remember that an antiques dealer is making an assessment of his stock based on his or her own knowledge, and no-one can be an expert in everything. Even experts are taken in by Victorian reproductions of eighteenth-century furniture, and gateleg tables of the 1930s, almost exactly like those made more than two hundred years earlier, will have acquired enough evidence of wear and tear to confuse matters. This is especially true if they were intended to confuse when they were made.

Although there will always be curios in furniture, one-offs that can stump anyone, the range of different articles (not styles, not individual pieces) is not very large. There are objects for putting things in or on, sitting on or lying on, for working on, objects to separate one part of a room from another (such as a screen), objects to hang things from (such as a hall stand), and mirrors. All furniture, unlikely as it may sometimes seem, was made for use, and this must always be kept in mind. A piece of furniture which doesn't do what it sets out to do is a mistake, a freak. We can see this in some of the foolish little writing tables which will take a diary or a notepad and nothing else.

The prices of furniture sometimes directly rate to usefulness, but sometimes not. Logically, a large wardrobe is better than a small wardrobe because the user can put more in it. But until recently large wardrobes have been anathema to the trade because they simply will not fit into a modern home, and they were bought, if at all, to cannibalise – to make use of the wood or the veneer. On the other hand, a large dining table is often far more expensive than a smaller one. Here it is a question of supply and demand. People who give dinner-parties to twelve or more people desperately want a large table; and if they are of the dinner-party-giving class, they are probably able to afford to pay several thousand pounds for what they want. 'Long' sets of chairs rise in price in a way which is almost algebraic. Two matching chairs – very little, four better, six much much better, and eight and more – in an auction room the sky can be the limit.

A carved oak settle of ambiguous date, the cost of which depends on who is bidding for it at auction. A piece of furniture that is either adored or disliked.

A classic piece of furniture, a George III satinwood and amboyna 'D'-shape card table about 1785, sold in 1988 for £2,530. Furniture such as this always appreciates in value.

A set of six Windsor chairs. The 'longer' the set the better, but make certain that they match.

A George III mahogany and crossbanded sideboard of about 1790. With this type of furniture it is possible that the brass gallery is removed and the side cupboards turned into drawers, making a dressing-table.

So if a price seems silly, it may not be. There may be a good practical reason.

If you buy from a second-hand shop or a junk shop you pay for what you get. No-one is going to guarantee your buy. It may be a bargain, it may be rubbish. It may be so badly damaged that even the expert restorer has decided that the hours of work he would spend in putting it right would still not make a decent piece of furniture. The quality of any furniture at a boot sale is so abysmal that anything halfway decent looks marvellous, so beware of spending money on something that may be 'useful' but turns out to be a home-made bit of carpentry that merits nothing other than being chopped up for firewood.

A good deal of furniture changes hands privately, sometimes between relations and friends, sometimes between strangers, the result of an advertisement in a newspaper or a card in a newsagent's window. It is possible to get splendid furniture this way, but the odds are that the vendor knows that the only way he or she is going to get rid of it is privately, that auction rooms have been approached and don't want it, and that outside advice has been taken about the price to put on the piece. So the 'old oak settle £35' may turn out to be a polished 1930s oak monstrosity. Or the 'four Windsor chairs' may be nondescript stick-backs made yesterday for the weekend cottage market. After one or two disappointments it is tempting to give up answering these advertisements, but don't. Similarly, if you are outbid at an auction time and time again, sit it out.

It is a good idea to have some idea of what you are going to do when you buy your piece of furniture. If it is for use, will it fit in with your existing furniture? Is it too large? If it is bedroom furniture, will it go up the stairs? Many beds have been bought at auction on impulse which simply will not go up a curved staircase; (if they are bought for strictly practical reasons, they can be cut in two and reassembled, but old beds have stout spiral springs and they can be a problem).

If one buys furniture for restoration and refurbishing, is the task too much? Many dealers, if they have a shed available at home or a room behind their shop, often buy furniture which they vow one day to do up and resell. But they rarely do. An old adage of the antiques trade is 'Don't buy work'. On the other hand, doing up damaged or distressed pieces of furniture by someone who knows the difference between a chisel and a drill can be a rewarding and profitable hobby and business. Most of the tools necessary can be found at the back of any garage.

So damaged or battered furniture can be deliberately sought and items in good condition can be ignored. The damage can be assessed. If there are large areas of veneer missing, is there any chance of getting veneer to replace it? Is it worthwhile stripping off all the veneer, and seeing what happens? Are there transformation possibilities? Can the whole thing be stripped, painted white, and experimented upon?

In such a case, the furniture does not have to be anything at all out of the way. You are just looking for raw material, a shape, an assembly of wood to work your wiles on. Going further, work out whether the degree of neglect is helpful. A piece of furniture, once painted, now only has the ghost of the existing paint on it; but this can be used as an undercoat in its present state, perhaps washed over with vinegar and water. And blotchy varnished surfaces can be painted onto directly using modern pigments.

Of course, antique furniture should never be subject to such treatment. It was in the past, when ignorance was rife. In the 1920s anything that stood still was likely to be given a coat of lacquer, usually black or 'Chinese red'. If in doubt, make enquiries. If you haven't a friendly antiques dealer nearby, approach an auction room. They are not going to turn down the chance of looking at what might be a possible find, and you are under no obligation to place it with them if you don't want to.

Many dealers make a very good living by buying furniture and putting it straight into auction, often buying from other auction rooms a few miles away. When selling at auction, of course, you pay their commission (on which there is VAT) and perhaps a selling premium. If you sell to an antiques shop or privately you don't, and will get possibly cash instead of a cheque. This is assuming you know how much you want for it. It is the rule rather than the exception for a private person selling to an antiques dealer to ask for an offer.

When selling in auction always put a reserve on the article, and take the auctioneer's advice. He is on your side, and will not put a low reserve so that it can be sold cheaply. If no reserve is put on it there is the chance that it will go cheaply, either to the dealers' ring or to a private person if the sale is poorly attended. Some people have an inflated idea of what their property will fetch in auction, and insist on too high a reserve, whereupon the goods fail to sell. If inexperienced in auction-room ways, do not go along and bid up your own goods to get a higher price, for you may misjudge your timing, be landed with your own goods and be obliged to pay auctioneers' commission!

Selling privately can be misleading. It is highly probable, especially if the furniture is high quality, that you will be selling to a dealer pretending to be a private buyer, purchasing goods at less than their real value by undermining the confidence of the seller.

Furniture Prices at Auction (1988)

Price guides are largely based on the prices obtained at auctions. It should be noted that these can be misleading for a number of reasons: the ring may be in operation, keeping values low; there may be keen collectors battling it out against each other, lifting the prices sky-high; a piece may be wrongly catalogued, and not challenged, possibly bought by someone who recognises what it is; the item may be suddenly and inexplicably in fashion, as happened in furniture with Pembroke tables, and is happening with big Victorian pieces, in porcelain with German nineteenth-century fairings, or in paintings with amateur ship portraits; the auctioneers may have missed out on publicity, with only the locals present to bid for some choice 'London' piece; awful weather may have kept out-of-town bidders away.

The following are real prices obtained in 1988 at a wide variety of auction rooms throughout the UK. The furniture is set out in roughly chronological order.

Elizabethan carved oak tester bed   *£4,300 Sotheby's, Billingshurst*

James I oak refectory table with three-plank top, frieze carved with vine leaves, on six bulbous legs with square feet with floor-level square-section stretcher   *£20,000 Boardman Fine Art, Haverhill*

Seventeenth-century oak gateleg table seating ten, 6ft 5in x 5ft 3in (1.92m x 1.57m), with baluster turned legs on square feet with double gate   *£3,400 Boardman Fine Art, Haverhill*

Oak court cupboard dated 1624, the upper section with carved scroll and roundel decoration, with four panelled doors with brass accessories and barley-twist supports   *£1,000 Mallams, Oxford*

Seventeenth-century pine box with iron bands and carrying handles, the interior fitted with compartments and drawers enclosed by lid and two two-panelled doors   *£660 Mallams, Oxford*

Seventeenth-century oak dole cupboard, comprising a double-arched open frieze over doors formed of balusters   *£3,600 Dacre, Son and Hartley, Ilkley*

Seventeenth-century oak coffer with some original and some later carving, with four arched panels separated by carved columns, with a double arched apron   *£1,550 Michael Newman, Plymouth*

Seventeenth-century walnut child's armchair with barley-twist turning and caned back and seat   *£2,100 Hamptons, Godalming*

Charles I oak press cupboard c1640 3ft 10in (1.17m) high x 3ft 1in (95cm) wide, with a recessed upper section with a door flanked by baluster turned supports above a base, decorated with painted sycamore panels   *£6,200 Sotheby's, Billingshurst*

Commonwealth oak refectory table 12ft 8in (3.86m) long with carved frieze, supported on six bulbous legs, with plain stretchers   *£10,000 Sotheby's, Billingshurst*

Seventeenth-century oak joined stool   £1,600 Hampton's, Godalming

Seventeenth-century oak dresser base, with three upper drawers, two lower drawers, flanked by cupboards, all with mitred mouldings   £12,500 Sotheby's, Billingshurst

Seventeenth-century oak court cupboard with carved panels   £2,500 Dacre, Son and Hartley, Ilkley

Seventeenth-century Dutch cedarwood chest of drawers with bone inlay, with deep geometric carving   £9,500 Sotheby's, Billingshurst

Charles II nailed hide coffer with nine drawers below a hinged cover, with brass carrying handles, on bun feet   £3,600 Sotheby's, Billingshurst

Seventeenth-century oak gateleg table with oval leaves, two drawers, on turned bulbous supports and stretchers, 5ft 4in (1.63m) wide when open   £2,400 Graves Son and Pilcher, Hove

Seventeenth-century oak inlaid armchair with crested toprail, panel back with turned side supports, high rectangular arm-rests on turned supports, ornate apron with pendulum drop, on four turned legs with splay feet   £4,600 Phillips, Ipswich

Seventeenth-century oak cabinet on bun feet with interior of eighteen drawers and dummy cupboard concealing secret compartment, behind carved and studded doors, and with carrying handles   £1,300 J. R. Parkinson, Son, and Hamer, Bury

Anglo-Dutch walnut double-dome bureau cabinet 7ft (2.13m) high   £20,000 Phillips, London

William and Mary fruitwood ten-seater gateleg table on spiral twist legs with plain stretchers   £8,800 Sotheby's, Billingshurst

William and Mary walnut oyster-veneer and floral marquetry cabinet on stand, with two large panel doors over a three-drawer stand   £11,000 Phillips, London

Late seventeenth-century oak chest-on-stand with four long graduated drawers on stand with stretcher and turned legs   £1,000 Hobbs and Chambers, Cirencester

Set of twelve Queen Anne walnut upholstered dining chairs c1710 with plain front cabriole legs   £36,000 Sotheby's, London

Queen Anne walnut lowboy with two drawers, shaped apron, and plain cabriole legs £6,200 Prudential, Guildford

Queen Anne burr elm bureau 2ft 3in (67cm) wide, two short and two long herringbone crossbanded drawers, with fitted interior with well, with replacement bracket feet   £7,400 Messenger May, Baverstock, Godalming

Queen Anne walnut veneered bureau cabinet   £15,000 Sotheby's, London

Queen Anne faded walnut chest with two short and three long herringbone-banded drawers   £1,200 Bonhams, London

Pair of Queen Anne parcel-gilt walnut stools c1710 on cabriole legs with pad feet   £31,000 Sotheby's, London

Six elm Windsor open arm elbow chairs with stick bars and central pierced splats, saddle seats, on turned legs with turned stretchers   £3,100 *Geering and Colyer, Tunbridge Wells*

George I quartered and crossbanded walnut lowboy 2ft 7in (77cm) wide, with three drawers, arched apron, on plain cabriole legs   £5,400 *Messenger May, Baverstock, Godalming*

George I walnut veneer bureau with five short and two long drawers on bracket feet   £1,650 *Eldon E. Worrall, Liverpool*

George I burr elm bureau bookcase with swan-neck pediment, bracket feet, three long drawers   £20,500 *Messenger May, Baverstock, Godalming*

Early eighteenth-century walnut chest of drawers, 2ft 4in (70cm) wide, with moulded quarter-veneered top, four graduated cockbeaded drawers, bracket feet, Victorian wooden knobs £19,500 *Phillips, Bath*

Set of ten George II Chinese Chippendale dining chairs   £63,000 *Sotheby's, London*

Chippendale period mahogany sideboard table in Gothic style 6ft 6in (1.92m) wide £40,000 *Phillips, London*

Pair of George II carved giltwood mirrors 4ft 2in (1.27m) tall and 3ft 1½in (93cm) wide   £2,200 *Wintertons, Lichfield*

George II rectangular folding-top walnut card table, with four square candle-stands, drawer, on cabriole legs with acanthus motif on knee, terminating in ball-and-claw feet   £2,600 *Holloway's, Banbury*

George II upholstered wing armchair with scallop front legs and later needlework upholstery   £2,200 *Holloway's, Banbury*

Eighteenth-century rococo mirror, gilt and pine open frame, richly carved   £3,000 *Russell, Baldwin and Bright, Leominster*

George III mahogany octagonal wine cooler with satinwood stringing   £1,400 *Lawrences, Bletchingley*

George III mahogany fan-inlaid and crossbanded demi-lune card table   £1,125 *McCartney's, Ludlow*

George III mahogany satinwood and tulilpwood sideboard inlaid with stained ivory neo-classical motifs on six fluted legs with spade feet   £80,000 *Sotheby's, London*

George III satinwood tea-caddy   £680 *Phillips, Bath*

George III mahogany double corner cupboard with dentil cornice, astragal glazed upper section, two-doored base on canted plinth   £3,400 *Woolley and Wallis, Salisbury*

George III mahogany dumb waiter with three graduated tiers, central turned column, and tripod legs   £1,100 *Mallams, Oxford*

George III mahogany night commode inlaid with burr walnut panels over two dummy drawers on chamfered legs   £1,300 *Woolley and Wallis, Salisbury*

George III oak dresser, with three-tier plate rack above a base with six drawers and two arched panel cupboards with ivory escutcheons   £2,700 *Prudential, Manchester*

George III walnut and feather-banded chest-on-chest, with moulded cornice, three short and six long drawers, on bracket feet   *£9,600 Phillips, Folkestone*

George III mahogany secretaire bookcase with swan's neck pediment, tracery glazed doors, with a secretaire drawer opening to reveal eight drawers and six pigeonholes, above a base with two panel doors, all on bracket feet   *£7,000 Phillips, Folkestone*

Pair of George III mahogany side chairs, with buttoned rectangular backs, square studded seat, and square-section legs with acanthus decoration   *£2,600 Bearne's, Torquay*

Pair of George III mahogany armchairs upholstered with floral tapestry on square chamfered legs   *£27,000 Christie's, London*

Eighteenth-century Dutch marquetry bombé bureau   *£6,500 Phillips, Bath*

Eighteenth-century oak dresser with raised open back   *£1,500 Coles Knapp, Ross-on-Wye*

Eighteenth-century oak bureau bookcase   *£1,600 Coles Knapp, Ross-on-Wye*

Pair of Sheraton-style mahogany demi-lune card tables with crossbanded top and frieze, on tapered square-section legs with stringing on spade feet   *£5,200 Graves Son and Pilcher, Hove*

Early nineteenth-century South German marquetry cabinet inlaid with holly, satinwood, and elm   *£15,500 Lawrences, Bletchingley*

Early nineteenth-century mahogany dining table extending to 8ft 10in (2.65m), with three extra leaves, on eight turned legs, the top having rounded corners, a reeded edge, and rosewood crossbanding   *£2,600 Holloway's, Banbury*

George IV mahogany cylinder bureau bookcase, with dentil cornice, glazed upper section, with fitted satinwood interior, on reeded turned legs   *£2,200 Prudential, Manchester*

Eight Regency mahogany dining chairs with padded seats, sabre legs, and urn motif on top   *£5,500 Phillips, Bath*

Regency rosewood tip-up circular table with satinwood crossbanding on central column set on a platform with four sabre legs on brass castors   *£8,800 Francis, Carmarthen*

Regency simulated rosewood library steps 5ft 3in (1.6m) high   *£2,200 Hy Duke and Son, Dorchester*

Regency rosewood folio stand on splayed legs with turned stretchers on brass castors   *£1,650 Prudential, Sevenoaks*

Regency mahogany oblong library table with cut-away corners, red leather insert, with four frieze drawers, on reeded legs with brass terminals and castors   *£6,100 Capes Dunn and Co, Manchester*

Regency mahogany breakfront secretaire bookcase with ebony stringing 9ft 5in (2.87m) high, 10ft (3.05m) wide   *£7,000 Phillips, Bath*

Pair of Regency open beech painted armchairs with caned seat and half-moon back with splayed turned front legs   *£4,000 Wintertons, Lichfield*

Regency burr maple tip-up circular table with segmented veneer, and tapering column of triangular section on platform with scroll feet   £11,600 *Bearne's, Torquay*

Regency mahogany window seat crossbanded in satinwood, with fluted back rails and supports and padded seat   £1,250 *Lawrence's, Bletchingley*

Regency mahogany Pembroke table   £400 *Laidlaws, Wakefield*

Set of Regency double-sided graduated shelves with cross-banded and inlaid apron on truncated splayed tapered legs   £6,800 *Bonham's, London*

Victorian oak four-poster bed in Jacobean style with heavy carving and grotesque canopy   £4,600 *Bigwood, Stratford-on-Avon*

Victorian burr walnut foldover card table, the shaped top with satinwood inlay, above a wavy-edge frieze on vase-shaped end supports and scrolled cabriole legs with a turned stretcher £1,200 *Biddle and Webb, Birmingham*

Victorian papier-mâché table with adjustable top inlaid with mother-of-pearl roses, on central support terminating in platform with three scroll feet   £320 *Lots Road Galleries, London*

Pair of marble-topped console tables in George III style with neo-classical ornament and simulated malachite frieze on tapering spade-foot legs   £4,800 *Bonhams, London*

Victorian mahogany library table 6ft 10in x 4ft 5in (2.07m x 1.35m), with rectangular top over frieze incorporating three drawers on either side, on four ornately carved legs with lion-head knees on paw feet   £16,000 *(bought for £5 in 1960s!) Phillips, Bath*

Victorian carved antler chair, with carved head with glass eyes, plain seat supported by four legs with hoof feet   £2,100 *Phillips, Bath*

Garden bench with a trellis back and square legs 6ft 6in (1.83m) wide, rotten throughout £250 *Wintertons, Lichfield*

Victorian oak parquetry and marquetry Arts and Crafts sideboard in style of William Burges, 7ft 10in (2.35m) wide with castellated three-mirror back above Islam-type drawers over base in Jacobean style, with two doors and central open division   £5,600 *Hobbs and Chambers, Cirencester*

Victorian burr walnut Canterbury with tray top, inlaid with boxwood and elaborately pierced   £1,100 *Christie's, South Kensington*

Set of six Victorian Hepplewhite-style mahogany dining chairs, with one carver, shield backs, serpentine fronted seats upholstered in hide, with fluted tapering square-section legs terminating in spade feet   £1,500 *Capes Dunn, Manchester*

Victorian rosewood writing and needlework box, with fold-top flap concealing two drawers, with bag, on angular twin supports with bobbin-turned stretcher   £1,050 *Hetheringtons, Amersham*

Victorian walnut Davenport desk with pierced brass gallery, two cupboard doors, and inset slope   £1,150 *Hetheringtons, Amersham*

German mahogany oval ornately carved firescreen c1860 raised on curved legs on ball-and-claw feet with castors   £950 *Louis Johnson, Morpeth*

Victorian open upholstered armchair with scrolled and carved part-upholstered arms on reeded legs   £880 *Sworders, Bishop's Stortford*

Victorian rosewood stool, with frieze decorated with flower heads, on cabriole legs   £760 *William H. Brown/Olivers, Sudbury*

Victorian burr walnut double bedstead, with triple panel arch headboard, turned ornate columns, and a footboard with a carved medallion depicting a paddle steamer and other ships   £660 *Capes Dunn, Manchester*

Victorian walnut, amboyna and maple credenza inlaid with floral motifs with gilt metal mounts, the centre cupboard flanked by shelved compartments with glazed curved doors £1,050 *Phillips, Folkestone*

Pair of Victorian Regency-style bergère armchairs with tapered front legs and pillar-fronted arm-rests   £1,700 *Phillips, Bath*

Flemish marquetry table c1860 with spiral twist legs in seventeenth-century style   £1,400 *Sotheby's, Conduit Street, London*

Victorian walnut double-fronted bookcase with bobbin-turned columns and beaded frieze 14ft 6in (4.42m) long   £2,300 *Phillips, Bath*

Oak centre table stained green designed by Philip Webb and George Jack for Morris and Co 10ft 5in (3.2m) long   £16,000 *Phillips, London*

White-painted bedside cabinet designed by Charles Rennie Mackintosh   £8,000 *Phillips, London*

Six oak dining chairs with tall rectangular slats and shaped rail on four square section legs with turned double stretchers designed by Charles Rennie Mackintosh for the Argyle Street tearooms, Glasgow   £34,000 *Phillips, London*

Ebonised sideboard inset with medievalist painted panels   £3,200 *Phillips, London*

Victorian aesthetic-style pitch-pine dressing table believed to have been originally sold by Liberty's   £50 *Bonham's, Chelsea*

Late nineteenth-century French mahogany cylinder desk with ornate raised top with fluted pillars, painted panels and drawers, with brass accessories, on narrow tapering legs   £2,600 *Warren and Wignall, Leyland*

Victorian mahogany breakfront bookcase 12ft 2in (3.71m) wide and 9ft 10in (3m) tall in Gothic style with six glazed doors with Gothic tracery, the base comprising six panelled arched doors, with exterior pillar supports   £6,000 *D. M. Nesbit, Southsea*

Victorian mahogany and marquetry commode in Sheraton style, with serpentine front, on tapering legs with spade feet   £4,000 *Hy Duke and Son, Dorchester*

Victorian brass bedstead   £650 *Bonham's, Chelsea*

Victorian rosewood dressing table in the form of a kneehole desk, with a divided panelled top which lifts to reveal a fitted interior   £4,000 *Sotheby's, London*

Victorian walnut medical cabinet in Arts and Crafts style with four panelled cupboard doors and tambour fall-front concealing compartments and drawers   £1,500 *Phillips, Plymouth*

Eight Victorian Chippendale-style mahogany dining chairs, including two carvers, with cabriole legs and ball-and-claw feet   £1,800 Phillips, Bath

Victorian Gothic pine ecclesiastical screen 17ft (5.18m) long 11ft 6in (3.5m) high   £2,700 Heathcote Ball, Northampton

Art Nouveau mahogany display cabinet, the moulded cornice above an open shelf joined by two satinwood inlaid panels flanking a leaded glass door enclosing a shelf, on eight tapering legs   £1,200 Christie's, Glasgow

American walnut Wootton (Wells Fargo) desk with maple fall flap   £4,050 Anderson and Garland, Newcastle-on-Tyne

Edwardian inlaid mahogany bonheur du jour with three drawers   £1,350 Laidlaws, Wakefield

Edwardian mahogany satinwood-banded kidney-shaped desk with leathered top, and nine drawers   £4,600 Phillips, Folkestone

Edwardian mahogany satinwood-banded games table incorporating roulette-wheel, baize-lined card table, counter wells, on square tapering legs with spade feet   £2,600 Phillips, Folkestone

Edwardian oak Jacobean-style refectory table 11ft 1in long (3.38m) with turned tapering legs joined by stretchers   £2,900 (bought for £20 about 1968!) Phillips, Bath

Edwardian satinwood stool with painted decoration   £320 Hy Duke and Son, Dorchester

Edwardian George III-style partners' desk, 6ft x 4ft (1.83m x 1.22m), one side with nine drawers, the other with three drawers and two cupboards, the top inset with gilt tooled green leather   £2,500 Norris and Duvall, Hereford

Edwardian mahogany linen press with satinwood inlay, with two panel doors above two long and two short drawers, the upper section converted for hanging clothes, with shelving removed   £1,050 Geering and Colyer, Tunbridge Wells

182ft (55.5m) run of oak wall panelling dated 1903   £1,600 Bigwood, Stratford-on-Avon

Edwardian mahogany and inlaid lady's writing desk with clock set in raised back above two serpentine drawers on tapered legs with spade feet   £1,300 Strides, Chester

Edwardian walnut wind-up extending dining table   £1,400 Lawrences, Bletchingley

Edwardian inlaid mahogany cabinet 6ft 2in (1.85m) high, 2ft 10in (85cm) wide, with two astragal glazed upper section over serpentine base, on six tapering legs   £2,000 Prudential, Manchester

Pair of Edwardian Carlton House writing tables   £6,200 Sotheby's, London

Edwardian inlaid mahogany breakfront combination wardrobe 9ft 5in (2.82m) tall   £2,100 Prudential, Manchester

Set of eight George III style mahogany dining chairs made c1910, including two carvers   £1,600 Giles Haywood, Stourbridge

Edwardian mahogany revolving bookcase with brass fitments on brass tripod base   £800 Andrew Grant, Worcester

Pair of pink damask upholstered two-seater sofas   £920 (estimate £20-£30!)   Bonham's, Chelsea

Set of seven 1920s Sheraton-style mahogany dining chairs   £660 Andrew, Hilditch and Co, Sandwich

1920s kingwood and gilt-metal vitrine, the cornice with gilt scroll mounts, the frieze sporting a central trophy, above glass shelving behind heavy bevelled glass door, on cabriole legs   £2,400 Thomas Love, Perth

1920s burr walnut dining suite of twelve pieces comprising eight chairs, a serpentine sideboard, an extending dining table, a display cabinet, and serving table   £2,200 Prudential, Manchester

Art Deco bird's eye maple upholstered three-piece drawing-room suite on tapered legs £1,250 Lots Road Galleries, London

Set of eight Art Deco burr walnut dining chairs including two carvers with satinwood fan-shaped backs, with seats upholstered in cream hide, and with tapered legs   £2,000 Norris and Duvall, Hertford

Three occasional Art Deco maple tables   £380 Phillips 2, London

Art Deco cocktail cabinet with peach mirror-glass doors opening to reveal fitted interior £1,000 Phillips 2, London

1930s Carlton House writing table with paw feet   £3,000 Sotheby's, Conduit Street, London

APPENDIX III

Historical Periods – A Brief Chronology

The Periods – Woods		The Periods – Styles	
Oak period	pre 1670	Jacobean (James I)	1603-25
Walnut period	1670-1730	Carolean (Charles I)	1625-49
Mahogany period	1730-1810	Commonwealth (Cromwell)	1649-60
		Restoration (Charles II and James II)	1660-89
		William & Mary	1689-1702
		Queen Anne	1702-14
		Georgian (George I, II, III)	1714-1811
		Regency (George IV)	1811-30
		William IV	1830-37
		Victorian	1837-1901
		Edwardian (Edward VII)	1901-1910

(Later monarchs have not given their names to furniture.)

There are styles within styles. The Chippendale style starts in 1754; Hepplewhite became known in 1788; Sheraton began publishing his designs in 1791. He died in 1806, but his designs were reissued in 1812, proving his importance. He had a great influence on Edwardian furniture. Robert Adam and his Neoclassicism was most important after 1765. Neoclassicism tended to displace Chinese and Gothic forms popularised by Chippendale in 1754. Thomas Hope (1769-1831) was very important in the designs of Regency furniture from 1807 onwards. In 1833 J. C. Loudon published the *Encyclopaedia of Cottage, Farm and Villa Architecture and Furniture* which went through eleven editions by 1867. He popularised quaint furniture and mechanical furniture.

The Gothic revival headed by A. W. N. Pugin (1812-52) began in the 1830s, and although it faded in the 1860s it still held an appeal for some. The most prominent exponent of the style was William Burges (1827-81), best known for his marvellous refashioning of the interior of Cardiff Castle (1865) and Castle Coch nearby (1875).

Art Nouveau in England dates from about 1880, and fizzled out shortly before World War I. The Aesthetic movement can be dated back to the early 1860s when Japanese art was rediscovered by E. W. Godwin (1833-86). He was very active from 1868, and was responsible for the Anglo-Japanese style and the use of ebonised wood.

It is difficult to say when the Arts and Crafts movement began. The seeds were sown by John Ruskin in the 1850s, William Morris began production in 1861, but the significant producers of Arts and Crafts furniture began later. The Century Guild was founded in 1882. The Art Workers' Guild was formed in 1884. The important firm of Kenton & Co was started in 1890 by Ernest Gimson, W. R. Lethaby and Ernest and Sidney Barnsley. Ambrose Heal published his first catalogue of 'plain oak furniture' in 1898. Gordon Russell began making furniture about 1914; from 1925 he was involved in furniture of great simplicity, from 1930 in modern furniture, and in World War II was largely responsible for the introduction of Utility furniture.

In 1925 there was an exhibition in Paris of modern decorative and industrial art, and loan pieces from this exhibition toured America. In 1927 the American store, Macy's, displayed modernistic pieces, and what became known as Art Deco (or alternatively the Jazz Style or the Modern Style) became commercialised.

Acknowledgements

The great proportion of colour pictures in this book has been supplied by Sotheby's Billinghurst, to whom I am very grateful. I should especially like to thank Tara Dewdney of Sotheby's Billinghurst for her help. Additional transparencies have been supplied by Sean Hickey of Torquay, to whom also many thanks are owed.

I am grateful to the following for the black and white illustrations: Phillips, London; Dee & Atkinson, Driffield, Yorkshire; Leigh Auction Rooms; Sotheby's Billinghurst; Dreweatt Neate, Donnington Priory; Abbot's Auction Rooms, Woodbridge; Holloways, Banbury; and Dacre, Son and Hartley, Ilkley, Yorkshire.

All other illustrations are from my own collection.

Further Reading

Andrews, J., **Price Guide to Antique Furniture** (Woodbridge 1969)
  Price Guide to Victorian Furniture (Woodbridge 1972)
  Price Guide to Victorian, Edwardian and 1920s Furniture (Woodbridge 1980)
Aslin, E., **Nineteenth Century English Furniture** (1962)
Boger, L. A., **The Complete Guide to Furniture Styles** (1961)
Buchanan, G., **Illustrated Handbook of Furniture Restoration** (1985)
Butler, R., **Arthur Negus Guide to Antique Furniture** (1978)
Chinnery, V., **Oak Furniture – the British Tradition** (Woodbridge 1979)
Edwards, R., **English Chairs** (1957)
  Georgian Furniture (1958)
Fastnedge, R., **English Furniture Styles** (1969)
Fleming, J. and Honour, H., **Penguin Dictionary of Decorative Arts** (1977)
Garner, P., **The World of Edwardiana** (1974)
Gloag, J., **Short History of Furniture** (1954)
Hayward, C., **Furniture Repairs** (1967)
  Staining and Polishing (1959)
Hayward, H. (ed), **Handbook of Antiques Collecting** (1960)
Hillier, B., **The World of Art Deco** (1971)
Hughes B. and T., **Small Antique Furniture** (1958)
Jervis, S., **Victorian Furniture** (1968)
Joy, E. T., **Country Life Book of English Furniture** (1968)
  English Furniture 1800-1851 (1977)
Laver, J., **Victoriana** (1966)
Macquoid, P. and Edwards, R., **Dictionary of English Furniture** (1954)
Moody, E., **Modern Furniture** (1966)
Musgrave, C., **Regency Furniture** (1971)
Osborne, H. (ed), **Oxford Companion to the Decorative Arts** (1976)
Ramsay, L. G. C. (ed), **Concise Encyclopaedia of Antiques 5 vols** (1955-60)
Roche, S., **Mirrors** (1957)
Rogers, J. C., **English Furniture** (1959)
Symonds, R. W., **Furniture Making in the Seventeenth and Eighteenth Century in England** (1955)
Toller, J., **Discovering Antiques** (David & Charles 1975)
Wood, V., **Victoriana** (1960)
Woodhouse, C. B., **Victoriana Collectors' Handbook** (1970)

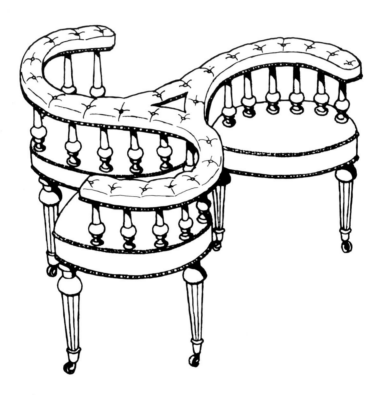

Index

Page numbers in *italic* denote illustrations